INDIAN BOTANICAL ART

INDIAN BOTANICAL ART
an illustrated history

MARTYN RIX

foreword by Sita Reddy

Kew Publishing
Royal Botanic Gardens, Kew

Lustre Press
Roli Books

© Roli Books 2021
Illustrations © The Board of Trustees of the Royal Botanic Gardens, Kew
unless otherwise stated on page 224
Foreword © Sita Reddy; Text © Martyn Rix

The authors have asserted their rights to be identified as the authors
of this work in accordance with the Copyright, Designs and Patents Act, 1988.

All rights reserved. No part of this publication may be reproduced,
stored in a retrieval system, or transmitted, in any form, or by any
means, electronic, mechanical, photocopying, recording or otherwise,
without written permission of the publisher unless in accordance with
the provisions of the Copyright Designs and Patents Act 1988.

Great care has been taken to maintain the accuracy of the information
contained in this work. However, neither the publisher nor the authors can be
held responsible for any consequences arising from use of the information
contained herein. The views expressed in this work are those of the authors
and do not necessarily reflect those of the publisher or of the Board of
Trustees of the Royal Botanic Gardens, Kew.

Published in all territories except India and N America by the
Royal Botanic Gardens, Kew, Richmond, Surrey, TW9 3AB, UK
www.kew.org

Kew Publishing ISBN 978 1 84246 722 0

British Library Cataloguing in Publication Data
A catalogue record for this book is available from the British Library.

Commissioning editor: Gina Fullerlove; **Copy-editor:** Michelle Payne;
Design: Sneha Pamneja; **Editor:** Neelam Narula
Pre-press: Jyoti Dey; **Production:** Lavinia Rao

Printed and bound in India
For information or to purchase all Kew titles please visit shop.kew.org/
kewbooksonline or email publishing@kew.org

Kew's mission is to be the global resource in plant and fungal knowledge,
and the world's leading botanic garden.

Kew receives about one third of its running costs from Government through the
Department for Environment, Food and Rural Affairs (Defra). All other funding
needed to support Kew's vital work comes from members, foundations, donors
and commercial activities including book sales.

Cover image: *Cheniella corymbosa* see page 99
Frontispiece: Sacred lotus, *Nelumbo nucifera*.
Artist unknown, for William Roxburgh, Calcutta, *c.* 1800.

CONTENTS

- Foreword by **Sita Reddy** — 6
- Preface by **Martyn Rix** — 10
- Introduction — 14
- Mughal Flower Painting — 30
- Dutch Trade in Kerala in the 17th Century and *Hortus Indicus Malabaricus* — 40
- Indian Botanical Artists of the 18th and 19th Centuries — 46
- The Scottish Surgeon-Botanists — 60
- Lady Impey and Sheikh Zain al-Din in Calcutta — 72
- William Roxburgh in Madras and Calcutta — 80
- Benjamin Heyne: A Naturalist in Madras — 98
- Adam Freer and Chunilall in Bengal — 102
- Claude Martin and the Lucknow Artists — 110
- Francis Buchanan-Hamilton and Haludar in Calcutta — 118
- The Calcutta Botanic Garden, Vishnupersaud, Gorachand and Nathaniel Wallich — 126
- John Forbes Royle and Vishnupersaud at Saharanpur — 142
- Hugh Falconer and the Calcutta Botanical Artists in Saharanpur — 156
- John Ferguson Cathcart and Joseph Hooker in Darjeeling — 166
- Robert Wight, Rungiah and Govindoo in Madras — 182
- Botanical Art in India Today — 202

- Bibliography — 220
- Index — 222
- Acknowledgements and Picture Credits — 224

FOREWORD

THE ROYAL BOTANIC GARDENS, KEW IS ONE OF THE GREAT botanic gardens of the Western world. Founded in the mid-18th century (as a private royal garden), it is today a thriving research centre for botanical science with one of the largest collections of plants and fungi, both living and dried, on the planet. But as with many colonial-era museums and archives in the UK, the last decade – partly inspired by the Black Lives Matter movement – has seen Kew engage in a process of self-critical acknowledgement of race and slavery in its own history, as well as an increasing sense of its role and responsibility as a public institution.

In 2020, George Floyd's murder in North America further propelled these conversations in the world's museums, all of which have had profound ripple effects on decolonisation practice in the UK's natural history museums. Kew's institutional response to this changing zeitgeist has been nothing short of transformative. Within the last six months, Kew has put out calls to decolonise its research collections, organised a conference *Botany, Trade and Empire* that foregrounded problematic colonial pasts and most recently, published a ten-year manifesto for change that aims to redress historical wrongs, diversify the workplace, reach under-served populations, and conserve biodiversity in what environmentalists call the 'sixth extinction'.

Kew's new book on Indian botanical art must be seen against this context and at this institutional juncture. Botany (and botanising) – far from being benign and politically neutral – were integral to the expansion of empire, providing ballast and lure to its swelling ambitions. Imperial botanical collections were built on the backs of spice trade routes, voyages of plant 'discovery', and plantation cultures – all systems of exploitation and extraction that plundered the world's natural resources for commercial profit and royal privilege. By the 18th and 19th centuries, as botany developed into a scientific discipline, Kew became an epicentre for the taxonomic documentation of plants gathered from the British Empire's far-flung colonies. And of these, Kew had a special relationship with India, empire's crown jewel. So much so that today it boasts unrivalled historical collections from the Indian subcontinent, including nearly a million herbarium specimens, extensive manuscript archives relating to East

India Company botanists and a unique collection of exquisite Indian botanical art, which forms the heart of this beautiful volume that you hold in your hands.

Given Kew's response to decolonisation, two questions can, and should, be asked of any new collections-based publication such as this. Does it tell the archive's untold stories? And does it acknowledge Kew's difficult past and collecting histories? The first is a question of archival purpose; the second, of provenance.

Even compared with other colonial-era natural history collections, the Indian botanical art at Kew bears a unique and double burden, and thus a unique and double responsibility, in the rewriting of hidden histories. No other Company botanical art genre anywhere owes as much to its native artists. Indeed, the very definition of *Kampani kalam* (as Company School was referred to in India, though the term itself has increasingly been dismissed as pejorative) signals that it was a quintessentially hybrid form – commissioned by East India Company surgeon-botanists but created entirely through the ingenuity of native Indian artists. And yet, these artists – some trained in Mughal and Rajasthani miniature traditions in north India, others in the vernacular craft traditions of the south – were rarely acknowledged or attributed. While the paintings were known, and continue to be catalogued, by the names of their Company commissioners – for example, the *Roxburgh Icones* – their artists, even their names, were invisible, their lives unsung. As we know from other imperial archives, *forgetting* indigenous makers is as much a part of archival construction as remembering. Reinserting the names of these forgotten artists thus becomes a way of correcting for profound archival erasure. This retrospective inclusion – literally, a re-membering of the archive, artist by artist, which in 21st century decolonisation practice remains one of the scientific community's biggest challenges – is one of this book's most valuable contributions.

A second contribution is archival reassemblage. If Kampani botanical art is a hybrid form, it is also a multi-genre and *dispersed* archive. In a colonial garden like Kew, three components of the botanical art story – the paintings themselves (aids to identify plants that did not

bristletips

Oxyspora paniculata (Melastomataceae)

Artist unknown, for John Cathcart, Darjeeling, *c.* 1850.

always survive overseas journeys from India), herbarium specimens (the *hortus sicci*, the dried garden), and manuscript archives (including Company botanists' papers) – were separated at time of accession and housed in different categories and places within Kew, thus furthering the dismemberment of a hitherto integrated archive. The paintings were filed taxonomically and geographically, by family, genus and species, which meant they were hard to access for the non-specialist. To re-tell the story of Indian botanical art through Kew's collections requires the reintegration of these dispersed archives, a mammoth research task of skill, diligence, and dedication, which places the moral burden, and rightly so, on the institution where they are held – on Kew itself. Here it is important to note that Henry Noltie, who pioneered this method of reassembly and research for Indian botanical art at the Royal Botanic Garden Edinburgh, has more recently extended his work to the Kew collection undertaking the bedrock upon which this book relies. With Henry's research across the Kew collections, both of these efforts – to refigure and to re-member the archive – are made visible in this gorgeous book. By reading across the archival grain, what emerges is at once a heroic story of the Indian artists who made the botanical art, as well as an institutional history of the imperial gardens in which this art collection grew, bloomed, and has been preserved.

Only a fraction of Kew's Indian collections has ever been shown to the public – whether through exhibitions, displays, or publications – and *Indian Botanical Art* aims to throw open the archive. Author Martyn Rix, editor of *Curtis's Botanical Magazine* and pre-eminent chronicler of botanical art whose many books have delighted readers around the world, has done a superb job in refiguring Kew's Indian drawings through this comprehensive and detailed review. And while there have been other publications of Indian botanical art that have attempted to restore the names of indigenous artists (including a special issue of *Marg* magazine, *The Weight of a Petal*, that I edited in 2018–19), this is the first to pull together Kew Gardens' Kampani botanical collections. Through research that weaves together extraordinary art with herbarium specimens and manuscript collections, through narratives that reinsert the artists' names, it offers a way in which to tell Kew's Indian botanical-art story from the ground up, through its artists and what W.J.T. Mitchell calls its 'migrant' art. Plants travel, and did travel, under colonial regimes, from colony to metropole. So did plant images. And indeed, given that the word *diaspora* has roots in botanical etymology, these diasporas of Indian botanical art give us the shifting backdrop – the proscenium stage and dramatis personae – for this book.

Collaborating with Delhi-based Roli Books suggests that colonial-era diasporic collections with difficult histories *can* return home to be repatriated in print or digital forms. At the tail end of the book are included several contemporary Indian botanical artists who show that although Kampani botanical art may have dwindled in importance with the advent of photography, today it is neither dead nor dying. These young legatees prove that, with dedication and discipline, botanical art can indeed enjoy a renaissance in the subcontinent. Subaltern artists not only speak but *draw* back to empire.

Two hundred years since the first botanical paintings were sent by ship from India to Kew Gardens, this book will be their first return to the subcontinent as a printed archive. In this sense, this small but significant volume is a giant step in the right direction. More than 70 years after gaining independence from the British Crown, the Indian post-colony inherited a hybrid botanical art tradition whose artists were invisible, then and now. With recognition of their role, past and present, can begin the urgent task of creating a poetics and a politics for the decolonisation of Indian botanical art. This timely and beautiful book seeds a promising future and a garden of archival possibilities. It is my honour and great privilege to write this foreword for Martyn Rix's *Indian Botanical Art* – a book based on Kew's collecting past that could well illuminate and shape its future.

Sita Reddy
Independent scholar and curator
Hyderabad

PREFACE

THE 18TH CENTURY SAW A RESURGENCE OF INTEREST IN THE natural world, and an almost obsessive attempt to list all species of plants and animals seen by European travellers to the Americas and to Asia. At the same time, sophisticated engraving techniques, lithography and other advances in printing created a demand for paintings which were published for patrons who could afford expensive illustrated books.

The young doctors who went to work for the East India Company had all been trained in botany as part of their medical course, and the few who were also keen botanists studied the unfamiliar plants they encountered, making dried specimens and commissioning local artists to make paintings of plants to keep an accurate record of the colours and details of the living plants. This was the background to this great flowering of botanical art.

Indian artists already trained and highly skilled in the Mughal, Rajasthani, Lucknow and other Indian miniature traditions were commissioned to make scientifically accurate paintings of plants, flowers and animals. Soon wealthy patrons, both Indian rajas and European visitors, as well as the East India Company itself, made collections of paintings of traditional medicinal plants and of the ornamental flowers and the birds and mammals they kept in their private gardens and menageries.

In 2015, I was asked to look at a collection of botanical paintings donated to the Royal Albert Memorial Museum & Art Gallery (RAMM) in Exeter by the Cresswell family. Among hundreds of paintings of English wildflowers, was a collection of Indian, mostly medicinal plants. With the help of Holly Morgenroth at RAMM and Professor Nandini Chatterjee from the University of Exeter, they were found to be unusually early, dating from the late-18th century, and painted by three artists from Patna who were among the first to work in this new Indo-European scientific style. Many of their paintings are signed with their names recorded as Sheikh Zain al-Din, Bhawani Das and Ram Das. These three also created wonderful portraits of birds, fish and some of the animals kept in Lady Impey's menagerie around 1780. Lady Impey lived in Calcutta with her husband and children between

1774 and 1783, when they returned to England. Much of her natural history collection is now in the Bodleian libraries in Oxford and in the Wellcome Collection in London.

When Joseph Hooker visited India around 1850, he met many of the East India Company botanists and admired the skill of their artists and the beauty of their collections of paintings. This led him to accumulate his own collection and add to it whenever he could, thus contributing to the great collection of paintings that are now preserved at the Royal Botanic Gardens, Kew. Hooker's collection, with later additions from the dispersal of the India Office Library, and acquisitions from other private sources, mean that Kew's collection is unrivalled in scope. Examples from the collection, which has remained almost unseen until now, form the basis of this book.

Henry Noltie has made a close study of many of the collections in Edinburgh and Kew, and their background in India, and it is his detailed work, gathering together individual botanists' collections dispersed through herbaria in Britain and India, which has enabled this book to be produced.

In recent years there has been a renaissance of botanical painting throughout India, with artists such as Hemlata Pradhan in Kalimpong, Nirupa Rao in Bangalore and Jaggu Prasad in Rajasthan, exhibiting around the world, and teaching botanical painting to a new generation, who are influenced by both Indian traditions and the modern European flower painting. Their work is shown here too, and demonstrates how the traditions begun in the 18th century continue to excite interest today.

Martyn Rix
Editor, *Curtis's Botanical Magazine*
Royal Botanic Gardens, Kew

INTRODUCTION

FLOWER PAINTING IN INDIA WAS FIRST MADE FAMOUS BY artists working for the Mughal Emperor Jahangir in the early 17th century; the paintings were in the miniature tradition, with beautifully embellished borders, but were decorative rather than scientific, and designed for pleasure rather than to help identification. A well-known image of a red tulip is thought to have been painted by Mansur, Jahangir's favourite artist, during a visit they made to Kashmir in the spring of 1620, and there are a few other paintings of irises, narcissus and other flowers from north-western India that are botanically accurate. In later paintings, however, the flowers became increasingly fanciful, some copied from flower illustrations in European books, some born in the imagination of the artist.

The first great flowering of Indian botanical painting took place in the late 18th and early 19th centuries, when Indian artists worked especially for surgeons employed by the English East India Company (EIC), and produced accurate drawings for both reference and scientific study. Initially, the botanists who worked for the Company were instructed to concentrate on economic and medicinal plants, but their enthusiasm for classification quickly led them to study the vast range of plants that they encountered, including those valued for their religious significance. Amateur enthusiasts for natural history, usually soldiers or civil servants, also made collections of plant and animal paintings, commissioning the same artists who worked for the Company surgeons. Many of the amateurs, who were not under the same pressure to concentrate on 'useful' plants, were also keen to record plants of ornamental value.

The EIC received its Royal Charter from Queen Elizabeth I in 1600, giving it a monopoly of British trade with the East Indies, China and Japan, at that time dominated by the Portuguese and the Dutch. The

Company's first trading station, or factory, on the Indian subcontinent was founded at Surat in Gujarat on the west coast in 1612, and a further trading station was established on the east coast at Fort St George, Madras (Chennai) in 1644. In 1668, the island of Bombay (Mumbai) was handed by the Portuguese to the English King Charles II as part of the dowry of his wife Catherine of Braganza, and the garrison was handed over to the EIC. Two years later, in 1690, the Company established itself in Bengal – at Fort William on the bank of the Hooghly river in Calcutta (Kolkata).

After the battle of Plassey in 1757 the EIC controlled most of Bengal, and for the next hundred years consolidated its power and expanded its trade throughout India, seeking new products which could be sold in Europe and eastern Asia. Dyes, such as indigo, printed cotton (chintz), sugar cane, tea, and spices were all important articles of trade; timber, and plant fibres for ropes for sailing ships were also exported. In addition, new crops were also introduced to India, notably, in 1861, *Cinchona* from Peru. The *Cinchona* plantations were mostly in the Nilgiri Hills near Ootacamund, and the quinine-containing bark was used for treating malaria. Tea plants were brought from China, though it was later discovered that tea was already growing wild in the forests of the Himalayan foothills in Assam.

Because of the expense of importing medicines, and the prevalence of diseases unknown or rare in Europe, there was also great interest in plant drugs, especially those used traditionally in Indian Ayurvedic medicine. The EIC employed doctors to treat both its European employees and its Indian soldiers (sepoys), setting up botanic gardens in different parts of India for the study and cultivation of useful plants. At that time, a course in botany was a compulsory part of the training of surgeons and doctors, which is why several of the surgeons,

INTRODUCTION 15

particularly those taught in Edinburgh, became pioneers of the study of Indian plants.

From the point of view of the directors of the EIC, based in Leadenhall Street, in the City of London, the study and promotion of medicinal and economic plants was of fundamental importance, as they could either be used profitably within India or exported to other Company trading stations around the world. Initially these were the main groups of plants studied by the Company employees, plants of purely botanical interest were added later.

trailing pea

Parochetus communis
(Leguminosae)

Vishnupersaud for John Royle at Saharanpur, *c.* 1828.

One species of this small, trailing pea is found throughout India, with a very similar species in East Africa. The plants are found in mountain woods, creeping along the ground.

Many native Indian plants, or those introduced in ancient times, were cultivated and illustrated because of their religious significance. The most familiar of these is the pink lotus, *Nelumbo nucifera* (see page 2), sacred to Buddha, which, though unrelated, looks similar to a waterlily. Also sacred in Hinduism is the peepal tree, *Ficus religiosa*, which is valued for its medicinal properties in treating a wide range of problems.

The first Western-inspired paintings of medicinal plants were printed in Holland in 1678, in *Hortus Indicus Malabaricus* by van Rheede tot Drakestein (see page 40). He was interested in all commercial aspects of the plants of the Kerala coast, and particularly in the spices and any plant with potential medicinal properties. Among those who contributed to the work were practitioners of Ayurvedic medicine, developed in India from around 5,000 years ago.

indigo
Indigofera tinctoria (Leguminosae)

Artist unknown, for William Roxburgh in Calcutta, *c.* 1800.

The plant from which indigo was produced.

Towards the end of the 18th century, the Company surgeons and doctors became interested in local medicines, seeking out medicinal plants and commissioning illustrations of them, for identification. In addition to studying the local plants, these doctors established experimental gardens in which to grow them, and, as noted by Alexander Gibson, hoped that medicines could be sold to the army to help defray the costs of the gardens. Robert Wight, for example (see page 182) spent many of his earlier years in India, attached to local regiments in the area around Madras, even when he was becoming well-known as a botanist.

Among any group of Indian botanical paintings collected by Europeans, a significant proportion of the plants have medicinal properties and were probably illustrated for this reason: this is particularly true of the plants in the apparently random Cresswell family collection in Exeter (see page 75), which probably dates from the end of the 18th century.

As well as studying and using local medicinal plants, the Company's doctor-botanists were also instructed to help cultivate well-known drug-producing plants for local use and for export. The most famous of these was opium – dried latex collected from the seed capsule of the opium poppy, infamous for its misuse but at the same time one of the few medicines that could arrest the worst symptoms of cholera. The first and most serious cholera outbreak started in India in 1817, then spread east through China and westwards as far as Europe, reaching London in 1832. Exports of opium were an important article of trade, notably to China where addiction became a serious problem; this has obscured its beneficial value as a painkiller and drug for treating stomach diseases and assuaging hunger pangs. Cannabis was also commonly cultivated, both as a relaxing smoke and as a fibre. Mortality from cholera, yellow fever and other tropical diseases was so great that it is estimated that in the early 19th century only one in ten of the Company's employees survived to make the voyage home.

From 1836, Robert Wight made a special study of senna, widely used as a laxative. The species commonly used, *Senna alexandrina,* was grown in Egypt as an annual, its dried leaves providing the drug. Wight, however, believed that some of the native species of *Senna*, used in local medicine, could be as effective as the commercial species, and cultivated in India for export.

This local knowledge continues today among country people in India. As Hemlata Pradhan (see page 213) observes when teaching local

cotton

Gossypium herbaceum or possibly *G. arboreum* (Malvaceae)

Artist unknown, for Claude Martin at Lucknow, *c.* 1780.

The cotton plant, long cultivated in India.

children: 'there [near Kalimpong], knowledge of the natural world and their surroundings come from the daily chores like cutting grass and collecting firewood from the forests. You ask them about "jungle medicines" and they will give you a list for broken bones, headache, jaundice, fever, high blood pressure, diabetes etc!'

Local Indian plants renowned for treating malaria included *Swietenia febrifuga*, now *Soymida febrifuga* (rowan bark), a tree in the family Meliaceae, which was studied by Dr William Roxburgh, and *Andrographis paniculata* (Kalmegh), a twiggy subshrub in the Acanthaceae family, which is used all over Asia for a variety of diseases. Turmeric (*Curcuma longa*) is another well-known and now very popular herb, with possible value as an anti-inflammatory. These and many other traditional herbal remedies are now being studied biochemically, to discover what biologically-active compounds they

INTRODUCTION 19

chilli pepper
Capsicum annuum (Solanaceae)

Artist unknown, for Adam Freer at Behrampur, *c.* 1810.

A native of South America, but now so commonly grown and used that it is hard to imagine Indian cooking without it.

might contain, and whether they can be proved to be beneficial in clinical trials.

In the mid-18th century, the Company changed from being a group of traders in some coastal ports to running parts of the country and trying to increase the income and prosperity of the peasant farmers by encouraging them to grow crops for sale and export in the Company's ships.

Plant dyes, particularly madder and indigo, were profitable early exports; printed cottons such as chintz and calico, associated with Calicut in India, became extremely popular in London from the late 17th century.

As a result, growing and experimenting with useful plants formed one of the main occupations of those employed as Company botanists. Roxburgh tested local plants and insects, notably the lac insect, whose larvae live on several plants including the pâlāsh tree (*Butea monosperma*) and produce a red resin. Its bark is said to have relaxant and aphrodisiac properties.

Indigo was probably the most important export from India in the 18th century. The original species was *Indigofera tinctoria*, which was grown both in Bengal and in the Northern Circars between Madras and Calcutta, but needed careful cultivation to be successful. Roxburgh tried other species of *Indigofera*, as well as the tree *Wrightia tinctoria*, as a tougher substitute; he also tested another species, *W. antidysenterica*, known as a medicinal plant but which also produced a good blue dye. Another aim was to identify new fibre plants, especially those that might be used for ship's ropes, as Russian hemp (cannabis) had become scarce because of the Napoleonic War.

Robert Wight was based around Coimbatore between 1842 and 1853, and tried to establish long-stapled American annual cotton in place of the short-stapled shrubby cotton native to India. For political and cultural reasons this was not successful. Henry Noltie quotes John Sullivan of the Madras Revenue Board: 'the cotton fabrics of India had been carried out to the highest perfection centuries and centuries before the cotton plant was known in America, it seems odd that we should be thinking now of importing people from America to teach the people of India how to cultivate, clean and collect their cotton.'

Forestry was another area in which the botanists became involved. By the late 18th century in some places in India the teak forests were

saffron

Crocus sativus (Iridaceae)

Possibly by Vishnupersaud, for John Royle, Saharanpur, *c.* 1828.

Saffron crocus, native of the Mediterranean, but grown in Kashmir since ancient times. The crimson stigmas of the flowers produce a valuable yellow dye, used for colouring cloth and rice.

dahlia

Dahlia sp. (Asteraceae)

Artist unknown, for Hugh Falconer, probably in Saharanpur, *c.* 1835.

Dahlias, popularly grown in India, are native of Mexico and were grown there as ornamentals before the arrival of the Spanish in the early 16th century.

seriously depleted, and the Company aimed to protect the supply of teak, used both for railway sleepers and for ship-building. New teak plantations were established, and cut and burn cultivation was actively discouraged or forbidden, which sometimes made the botanists and foresters unpopular with the local inhabitants. In 1856, Hugh Cleghorn was appointed conservator of forests for southern India, and later inspector-general of forests, and the Imperial Forest Department now in Dehradun was established in 1864.

The relief of periodic local famines, and the production of new food sources for the indigenous population, was one of the main aims of the rulers of India. Failure of the monsoon and the subsequent shortages of rice and millet, the staple grain crops, could quickly cause serious famine, even in small areas. The inability to move food from one area to another, except by slow bullock cart, meant that famines could be quite local, but still impossible to alleviate.

spider flower

Cleome houtteana (Cleomaceae)

Artist unknown, for John Cathcart in Darjeeling, *c.* 1850.

Grown as an ornamental in India, but native to South America.

Another focus was to identify products that could be grown in India and exported around the world. Herbs and spices were the most important, as they were high in value and could be transported in a dried state.

Introduced food plants tested at Dapuri garden, south-east of Bombay, included maize, oats, rye, Russian wheat, 'Abyssinian grain' possibly tef (*Eragrostis tef*), niger seed (*Guizotia abyssinica*), *Amaranthus frumentaceus*, and groundnuts; there are also many paintings of beans, such as the American Lima bean (*Phaseolus lunatus*).

There were also Indian plants such as tamarind, cashew-nut, cucumbers and melons (*Cucumis* species). Among the edible herbs and spices tested at Dapuri were black cardamom (*Amomum subulatum*), ginger (*Zingiber* species), coriander (*Coriandrum sativum*), cinnamon (*Cinnamomum*), and pepper (*Piper* species). A number of these had been grown in parts of India for many years, while others were newly introduced.

Other edible plants commonly cultivated, such as sugar cane or the large starchy tubers of *Amorphophallus*, are occasionally illustrated, with more familiar vegetables such as garden peas and various beans. Spices had always been an important export from Kerala. Since before the time of the Dutch and Portuguese traders, traditional crops for export included cardamoms (*Elettaria cardamomum*) to Arabia and black or white peppercorns and cinnamon (*Piper nigrum* and *Cinnamomum verum*) to Europe.

It is interesting that a common sight in India today is the making of garlands with the yellow flowers of African marigolds (*Tagetes patula*). Other varieties of *Tagetes*, *Zinnia* and *Cosmos* are commonly seen on roadsides and in gardens throughout the country. Few people know that these are all introductions from Mexico and South America, probably brought to India by the Portuguese in the 16th century. They have grown so well in India, where the climate of wet summer and dry winter is similar to that in Mexico, that they appear native.

The introduction of new garden plants was another aim of the Company botanists and the botanic gardens established around India. Some of the most common flowering trees and climbers in Indian gardens were introduced in the early 19th century, such as the goldmore tree (*Delonix regia*) from Madagascar, discovered in 1828, the flaming trumpet (*Pyrostegia venusta*) from Brazil, introduced from England in 1815, and poinsettia introduced from Mexico in

Indian frankincense

Boswellia serrata (Burseraceae)

Artist unknown, for William Roxburgh, Calcutta, *c.* 1800.

Native on dry hills in much of India and into Pakistan. Roxburgh named this after Dr John Boswell, a Scottish botanist and doctor with whom he lodged while a student in Edinburgh.

1828. *Ipomoea quamoclit*, now common and widely used in India and South-East Asia in traditional medicine, is also a Mexican native, but an earlier introduction, possibly in the 17th century. Early illustrations by Indian painters of these plants in botanic gardens, when they might have been new and special, can give us a definite date by which they had been cultivated in India.

Until the 20th century, illustrated printed books were extremely expensive, requiring an artist to produce the original drawing, an engraver to make the line drawing on a copper plate and then artists to hand-colour the printed engraving. Indian miniature artists were, and still are, excellent copyists. They were soon producing illustrations of plants, often in multiple copies, for reference, under the supervision of European botanists, and using European illustrations as models.

There are surviving collections of Indian paintings in many private collections in India and in Britain, but many of those drawn for the

Indian shot
Canna indica (Cannaceae)

Artist unknown, for Nathaniel Wallich in Calcutta, 1828.

Though common in India, and throughout the tropics, it originates from the southern USA to northern Argentina. The name Indian shot refers to the hard round lead-coloured seeds.

Company surgeons are in Britain, in the libraries of the Royal Botanic Gardens, Kew, the Natural History Museum in London, and the Royal Botanic Garden Edinburgh. In India, the main collections are in the former Calcutta Botanic Garden (now the Acharya Jagadish Chandra Bose Indian Botanic Garden, Kolkata), the Lalbagh collection in Bangalore (Bengaluru), and the Thanjavur Sarasvati Mahal Library.

These Indian botanical paintings, as well as bird and animal paintings and scenes of Indian life, are traditionally known as Company School (or *Kampani kalam*). This term is now questioned both for its focus upon the European employees of the EIC who commissioned the paintings, rather than the artists themselves, and for concealing the considerable stylistic diversity of the artworks. Furthermore, similar

flame-of-the forest, dhak tree or pâlāsh

Butea monosperma (Leguminosae)

Artist unknown, possibly Sheikh Zain al-Din, *c.* 1800.

This is one of the trees that are host to lac insects (*Laccifer lacca* or *Kerria lacca*); they feed on the ruby-coloured gum and their eggs can be crushed to make a dye. In the 1790s the East India Company hoped that this might be used as a substitute for cochineal but it did not prove suitable. True cochineal is produced by crushing insects that feed on the Mexican prickly pear cactus.
© Royal Albert Memorial Museum & Art Gallery, Exeter City Council.

works produced in other parts of the East Indies, China and Japan are also confusingly termed Company School.

The Calcutta Botanic Garden, the pre-eminent botanical institute in India, was founded in 1786 at Sibpur on the right bank of the Hooghly river just below Calcutta, but there were soon other gardens around India, and most of them survive to this day. The Lal Bagh in Bangalore was taken over by the Company from Tipu Sultan in 1799 and the garden at Saharanpur, in Uttar Pradesh near Dehradun was taken over as an experimental garden in 1817.

The most famous of those who published illustrated works on the Indian flora during this period was Dr William Roxburgh, whose *Plants of the Coast of Coromandel* (1795–1819), started while he was based in coastal Andhra, is particularly splendid. Roxburgh later moved to superintend the Calcutta Botanic Garden, where he was followed by Dr Nathaniel Wallich, whose *Plantae Asiaticae Rariores*, also with 300 superb hand-coloured plates, was published between 1830 and 1832. While based in Saharanpur, John Forbes Royle published his *Illustrations of the Botany of the Himalayan Mountains* (1833–1840). The great botanical artist Vishnupersaud made illustrations for both Wallich and Royle – arguably the most beautiful of all the illustrations of Indian plants ever made. Of the Scottish botanists, Dr Robert Wight (1796–1872) was the most prolific, commissioning and publishing hundreds of detailed scientific drawings of plants, mainly from southern India, including *Spicilegium Neilgherrense* (1846 and 1851) and *Icones Plantarum Indiae Orientalis* (1838–1853). The drawings for these works were by Rungiah and his pupil Govindoo.

These books were engraved or lithographed from the original paintings by Indian artists, and although printed in small editions and correspondingly rare, they can be found in libraries in India and elsewhere. But in addition to these published illustrations, Roxburgh, Wallich and Wight commissioned large numbers of plant paintings that have remained unpublished and almost unknown.

A second high point in Indian botanical art has occurred much more recently, and there is now a lively interest in the subject (see page 202). In the absence of specialist courses at home most Indian botanical artists, such as Hemlata Pradhan and Nirupa Rao, have travelled abroad for training; but as a new generation of young and talented painters have returned to India, there is now a far greater chance for aspiring botanical artists to obtain instruction locally. A parallel group of artists has been trained in India (particularly in Jaipur, Rajasthan), using traditional techniques of miniature painting as handed down from the artists trained at the courts of Mughal emperors. These skills are well suited to the demands of botanical painting, even if usually put to more purely decorative ends. Thanks to the internet, and international support and exhibitions, the work of this new generation of artists in all its diversity has deservedly become more widely known, and paintings and prints can be sold to collectors anywhere in the world.

MUGHAL FLOWER PAINTING

THE SURVIVING EARLY MUGHAL PAINTINGS, DATING FROM the 16th century, are mostly from Central Asia, from Bukhara to Afghanistan. Flowers are shown both in a wild setting, to accompany hunting scenes, and in a garden setting, particularly following the example set by Babur who laid out gardens in Kabul after his capture of the city in 1504. An illustration from a manuscript of the life of Babur, compiled by order of Akbar, is now in the Victoria and Albert Museum in London; it shows Babur supervising the planting of flower beds, in a garden divided by streams, flowing into a square tank, surrounded by fruit trees and evergreens.

Though Babur continued his conquests into India, where he died in Agra in 1530, he instructed that his body be buried in the Bagh-e Babur in Kabul, which took place in 1544. Babur's successors continued his love of gardens and flowers, none more so than his great-grandson Jahangir, who reigned from 1605 to 1627. When he was not fighting, Jahangir both visited gardens and commissioned paintings of flowers, birds and animals. One of his famous paintings, and at the same time one of the earliest surviving portraits of a single flower in Mughal art, is of a tulip, now in the Maulana Azad Library, Aligarh Muslim University. It is signed 'Jahangirshahi, the work of the slave of the Presence-Chamber, Mansur Naqqash'. Mansur began his career as an illuminator in the court of Akbar, but his finest plant and animal paintings were created for Jahangir.

In his journal Jahangir described how he visited Kashmir in autumn 1607 and admired the flowers but did not go there again until the spring of 1620 or 1621. He was fascinated by the crown imperial (*Fritillaria imperialis*): 'there was one strange flower in particular, with an odd shape. It had five or six orange-coloured flowers blooming with their heads down, and several leaves were poking out from *among* the flowers… It was something like a pineapple.' Mansur was in Jahangir's entourage and is said to have painted more than a hundred flowers on this visit, possibly including his tulip. Red-flowered tulips

Red tulip signed by Mansur, painter of King Jahangir, c. 1620. Habibganj Collection, Maulana Azad Library, Aligarh Muslim University, no. 60-1-ba-3. Photograph Ebba Koch.

Page from Gulshan album, flower studies, with upper left panel of lilies and other bulbs copied from a European herbal with irises and violets beneath. Signed by Mansur, *Jahangir Shahi, c.* 1615. Golestan Palace Library, Tehran: No. 1663 p.103.

grow in the saffron fields around Srinagar and have been identified as *Tulipa montana.* A rather similar painting of an iris, with a bird and a dragonfly, is in the Nasir al-Din Shah album, Golestan Palace Library, Tehran. With its blue flowers, flat leaves and branched stem, it could be *Iris kashmiriana.* It is very sad that these are perhaps the only two to have survived out of the hundred flowers that Mansur painted. Many other flowers accompany his bird paintings: a pair of bustards are shown with *Sophora mollis*, and a pair of pheasants have a border of many flowers including poppies, roses and red lilies.

There is no doubt that another painting signed by Mansur is derived from a European original. This is also in the Nasir al-Din Shah album and shows a whole page of different lilies, with fritillaries, a grape hyacinth and a rosebud, but the colouring is fanciful because Mansur did not know the flowers himself. This page has been shown to be copied from an engraving in the florilegium published by the engraver Adriaen Collaert in Utrecht in around 1589. Collaert, however, was not the originator of these images, because some of them had appeared earlier in Clusius's *Rariorum aliquot stirpium etc.* published by Plantini in Antwerp in 1583 and used again in Gerard's *The Herball*, published in London in 1597.

The printer of Gerard's herbal, John Norton, obtained the images from the Dutch printer, Nicolao Bassaeo, who was based in Frankfurt-am-Main, and many of them had also been used in Tabernaemontanus's *Eicones Plantarum* of 1590. It appears likely that Mansur had access to a copy of Collaert's florilegium and used it to practise drawing flowers in the European style.

There are many other notable single portraits of plants from the Mughal period including a beautiful and realistic field poppy (*Papaver rhoeas*) in the Small Clive album in the Victoria and Albert Museum. This album also contains plants copied from European originals, notably a martagon lily (*Lilium martagon*) derived from the drawing in Pierre Vallet's *Le Jardin du Roy* (1608). A flower of the native Indian glory lily (*Gloriosa superba*), in an album in the Bodleian Library in Oxford dating from about 1650, was most probably drawn from life, as it only appeared in Europe at the end of the 17th century.

One of the distinctive features of this style of painting is the decorative borders that show a range of different flowers. These could have been influenced by the floral borders in Christian prayer books known as 'Books of Hours', popular in the Netherlands and northern Europe in the 15th and 16th centuries and known to have been in the court

MUGHAL FLOWER PAINTING

Fragment of pashmina shawl border, Kashmir, c. 1650. Collection: Jagdish and Kamla Museum of Indian Art, Hyderabad.

Calligraphy panel by Mir'Ali in Bukhara, possibly in the 1520s. Illumination signed by Dawlat, c. 1615. Borders, reign of Shah Jahan. Victoria and Albert Museum, London: IM12a-1925.

library. These floral borders can be seen in 17th-century paintings in Iran and across Asia into India.

The Taj Mahal was built between 1631 and 1648 by Shah Jahan for his beloved wife, Mumtaz Mahal, who died in childbirth in 1631. The wonderful marble decorations on its walls feature representations of many different flowers, both in white marble and in coloured *pietra dura* – inlaid stone in the Italian style. Tulips, lilies, irises and crown imperials are easily recognisable, and were probably copied from an earlier album of flowers. The flower-filled urns shown in some of the marble panels may even have been copied from Collaert's florilegium.

A most beautiful album, now in the British Library, was created for Dara Shikoh, the eldest and favourite son of Shah Jahan and Mumtaz Mahal, a cultivated patron of the arts and enlightened mystic. He was born in 1615 and in 1633 married his cousin Nadira Banu Begum. He gave her the album in 1641, but it is said to have been assembled earlier, between 1630 and 1633. In 1659 Dara Shikoh was murdered by his younger brother, Aurangzeb, who had seized the throne from his father and proceeded to institute a period of harsh Islamic Sharia

34 INDIAN BOTANICAL ART

Detail of flower art; polished marble with stone inlay, Red Fort in Agra. Igor/123RF.com.

→

Naturalistic tulip and hollyhock flower motifs in marble relief, on the facade of the Taj Mahal, Agra. Late 1630s.
Laddawan Hengtabtim/ 123RF.com.

rule and high taxation. The album survived in the Mughal royal collection, and its provenance is clear, even though attempts were made to erase Dara Shikoh's name from its pages.

The only named artist of the Dara Shikoh album was called Muhammad Khan, possibly from Burhanpur in the Deccan, who signed a painting in 1633–34. The page shows several flowers, all very stylised, including dark blue irises, pink roses, a yellow double African marigold, a possible scarlet pimpernel and, perhaps, a dark-purple-flowered larkspur. The painting of a man in an orange coat and green turban, pouring wine, shows a dish of pomegranates, a blue and white vase of flowers, and a border of irises, tulips, anemones and other flowers. A lady stands by a clump of *Narcissus tazetta*, holding a

single blossom in her hand. Other paintings show crown imperials and martagon lilies, but with unnatural colours, again suggesting that they were derived from a black-and-white print.

Following the death of Shah Jahan, and under the rule of Aurangzeb, Mughal patronage of art declined. Most of the paintings that were produced were miniatures of court life or hunting scenes, particularly in the provincial princely courts of Rajasthan, such as Jodhpur and Jaipur. Few if any plant portraits survive from this period, though there are paintings that show trees as backgrounds to hunting scenes or paintings of gardens. Flower paintings also survive as frescoes, notably on the walls of the desert palace in Nagaur, formerly the site of an elaborate water garden. Among the thousands of paintings in the Mehrangarh museum in Jodhpur are many showing gardens with colourful beds of flowers. These include plants that must have been brought by Portuguese traders from Mexico and the Canary Islands, and many are still common in Rajasthani gardens: white shrubby daisies (*Argyranthemum* species), yellow and orange marigolds (*Tagetes patula*), and zinnias (*Zinnia elegans*) in a characteristic mixture of orange, red, pink and purple. All these can be identified in paintings of scenes of the Rajasthani court at Jodhpur in the 17th and 18th centuries.

Flower studies including marigold, iris, chrysanthemum, pimpernel, rose and possibly a dark purple spur. Folio from Dara Shikoh album, attributed to Muhammad Khan, 1630-33. Add. Or. 3129 f.67v.
© British Library Board. All Rights Reserved / Bridgeman Images.

DUTCH TRADE IN KERALA IN THE 17TH CENTURY AND *HORTUS INDICUS MALABARICUS*

THE FIRST GREAT ILLUSTRATED BOOK ON INDIAN PLANTS WAS printed in Holland in 12 volumes between 1678 and 1693. The Dutch East India Company (Verenigde Oostindische Compagnie or VOC) was the largest company trading between eastern Asia and Europe in the 17th century and had an important post at Cochin in present-day Kerala on the south-western coast of India. Silk, cotton and spices were then the main items of trade, and Kerala is still a significant producer of pepper and cardamom.

The Dutch governor, Hendrik Adriaan van Rheede tot Drakestein (1636–91), had entered the service of the VOC as a soldier aged 20. Later he fought against the Portuguese to control the trade of the northern Malabar coast, and by 1669 had become commander of the Dutch forces in Malabar where he established a good relationship with the Raja of Cochin. Like many Dutch of his time, he was interested in plants for ornament, as well as for their medicinal uses, and was particularly keen to study and codify the traditional medicines of southern India. The result of his interest was the magnificent *Hortus Indicus Malabaricus*, which included wild and cultivated plants, shrubs and trees, and is illustrated by bold engravings made in Holland based on drawings made in India by Dutch artists. The plant names are given in Latin, Sanskrit, Malayalam and Konkani, with the Malayalam name also in Arabic script. These are supported by an extensive Latin text, translated from the Indian languages by two priests, Fr Johannes Casearius and Fr Mathew of St Joseph, with detailed botanical descriptions by the botanists Jan Commelin, Paul Hermann and Johannes Munnicks.

The ethno-medical information was extracted from palm leaf manuscripts by a famous practitioner of herbal medicine named Itty Achudan, a native hereditary Malabar physician and expert on the Ayurvedic properties of plants. Three Brahmin priest physicians,

Appu Bhat, Vinayaka Pandit and Ranga Bhat were also consulted. In all a team of nearly 100 people worked on various aspects of the book, encouraged by the ruling Raja of Cochin and Zamorin of Calicut. The manuscript and illustrations were prepared in Cochin, and the first volume appeared just before van Rheede returned on a visit to Holland in 1678 taking the rest of the manuscript with him, having had copies made in case he was shipwrecked. His departure from Kerala appears to have been caused by jealousy between the Dutch in Ceylon (Sri Lanka) and his own staff in Kerala. He left Europe again in 1684, with instructions to check on, and combat, corruption among VOC employees in the Cape, Ceylon and Malabar, but died at sea between Bombay and Surat in 1691, poisoned, some say, by his own men.

As the first substantial book on the Indian flora, *Hortus Indicus Malabaricus* was very influential. Although it predates the great Swedish taxonomist Linnaeus's reform of botanical nomenclature he spoke highly of its accuracy, commenting in the second edition of *Genera Plantarum* (1742) that, 'I have had no trust in any author, excepting the very celebrated Dillenius in *Hortus Elthamensis*, [and] Rheede in *Hortus Malabaricus*, whom I have observed to be accurate.'

Many of van Rheede's names were taken up by Linnaeus and are still in use today, notably *Basella*, the Malabar spinach. Others, are used as specific names, for example the tree now called *Magnolia champaca* and the pepper *Piper betle*. As will be seen later, Francis Buchanan-Hamilton in the 1820s wrote a commentary providing identifications of the species in the light of current knowledge.

An English translation of *Hortus Indicus Malabaricus* by Professor K.S. Manilal of the University of Calicut, published in 2003, has made the text accessible to English readers, and a Malayalam version has also been published recently in Kerala.

mango tree
Mangifera indica (Anacardiaceae)

Unknown Dutch artist for van Rheede tot Drakestein, *Hortus Indicus Malabaricus* (1678–93). Part 4, tab. 2.

The mango has been cultivated in India for over 2,000 years for its fruit. The scientific name was published by Linnaeus in 1753, quoting this picture.

bitter melon

Momordica charantia (Cucubitaceae)

Unknown Dutch artist for van Rheede tot Drakestein, *Hortus Indicus Malabaricus* (1678-93). Part 8, tab. 9.

A climbing annual popular as a vegetable.

INDIAN BOTANICAL ARTISTS OF THE 18TH AND 19TH CENTURIES

MANY EMPLOYEES OF THE ENGLISH EIC WHO CAME TO MADRAS and Bengal in the late 18th century were as amazed and fascinated by local costumes as they were by the plants and other aspects of natural history. They also discovered that there were talented artists available locally who were happy to copy Indian miniatures for sale and, at the same time, to draw portraits and local scenes in a more European, or hybrid Mughal-European style. Schools of painting thus grew up near the main centres of administration where European patrons were stationed and around Company botanic gardens, notably in Calcutta.

The Europeans wanted their natural history paintings to approximate to the style of 18th-century French and English artists such as Redouté, Curtis, Catesby and Sowerby, so the Indian painters had to learn to work on a larger scale, making the plant paintings at least near life-size, and in a more naturalistic style. In some early paintings, notably some of Claude Martin's collection from Lucknow, the plants are very formalised, and some of the parts are drawn non-naturalistically.

The earliest flower paintings in this hybrid style, dating from around 1772, were made for European patrons and commissioned by Dr James Kerr, a Scottish surgeon stationed in Bengal. It has been found that some of Kerr's paintings are by the artist Bhawani Das. In 1775, when Lady Impey arrived in India and established her estate and garden near Calcutta, she began to commission paintings of the natural history species she collected. The names of Lady Impey's three artists are known as she scrupulously recorded them: Sheikh Zain al-Din, Bhawani Das and Ram Das, all of whom came to Calcutta from Patna. They painted the birds, animals and flowers in her collection, and Bhawani Das also painted snakes and fish. The same three artists produced other paintings, including plants, for Henry Creighton, who almost certainly commissioned the Indian flower paintings in the Cresswell family collection (see page 73), probably in Calcutta after 1783, when Lady Impey left India.

A collection of particularly accomplished paintings in the Kew collection are attributed to the artist Manu Lall, and were commissioned by Richard Parry (1776–1817). Parry was sent as Resident to Bencoolen in Sumatra in 1807, and there Manu Lall illustrated cultivated plants such as the coffee bush, and wild plants such as the strange pitcher plant *Nepenthes ampullaria*, which has whorls of small pitchers rather than the large single pitcher found in most species of *Nepenthes*. It seems likely that Manu Lall accompanied Parry to Sumatra as his artist. Another artist named Chunilall, possibly of the same family from Patna, painted animals and plants, a few of which are in Adam Freer's collection and are of similar date. It appears that there was a large family of Lalls, as several artists with this surname are noted on paintings collected by Adam Freer.

William Roxburgh arrived in Madras in 1775. Excellent though they were, we do not know the names of any of the artists who worked for him. He started to commission drawings in south India, and by 1790 was sending paintings to Sir Joseph Banks in London for comment. Roxburgh's chief artist started painting flowers for him in Madras in around 1789 and moved with him to Calcutta in 1793. We know that this artist died in 1814, as an application was made to the Company for a pension for 'the head painter's widow'; his name, however, was still not recorded.

Roxburgh's successor in Calcutta, Nathaniel Wallich, employed several botanical artists; their names are known because, unlike Roxburgh's, they were acknowledged when their drawings were published in London. Vishnupersaud, who produced large and wonderful paintings, worked for Wallich in Calcutta and on travels to Nepal and Burma, and his skill is such that he must have been employed as a botanical artist long before Wallich took over in 1817. Other artists employed by Wallich whose names are known were Gorachand and Ramchand, whose drawings were first published as etchings in 1820 in an article in *Asiatic Researches* entitled 'Descriptions of some rare Indian plants'.

Portrait of an artist from James Skinner's *Tashrih al-aqvam* (Account of the Castes). Late Mughal, 1825. © British Library Board.

When Wallich went on a four-year leave to Europe in 1828, Vishnupersaud and the other Calcutta Botanic Garden artists worked for John Forbes Royle in Saharanpur, and many of their paintings were published in Royle's *Illustrations of the Botany of the Himalayan Mountains,* which appeared in parts between 1833 and 1840. The Calcutta botanical artists, including Luchman Singh, Bhagoban, Kassim Ali, Bhookunt and Rajbulub, continued to work at Saharanpur for Royle's successor Hugh Falconer. Falconer was superintendent in Saharanpur from 1832 to 1841, and then of the Calcutta Botanic Garden from 1848 to 1855. Luchman Singh also became skilled in lithography and worked with Bhagoban on the illustrations for William Griffith's *Posthumous Papers*, published in Calcutta in the 1840s.

Another botanist who gave full acknowledgement to his artists was Robert Wight, who worked in Madras from 1819 until 1843. Wight's intention was different from the other botanists, in that he planned to publish the drawings himself in India, and at an affordable price, rather than hope that the Company would produce a magnificent colour-plate book in London. He also wanted to publish as many illustrations as he could to assist other botanists with identification, and to produce a comprehensive flora of south India. His drawings are therefore smaller, of quarto rather than folio size, with great emphasis placed on enlarged floral dissections.

Wight trained two artists, Rungiah and Govindoo, who between them produced over 4,000 plant illustrations, of which 1,445 were published. Rungiah began to work for Wight around 1826 and is known to have worked both in the studio and in the field, making sketches and colour notes for later completion. He worked fast and could produce '10 or 12 drawings a month'. Wight has left an interesting account of Rungiah's method of working 'by laying the plant on the paper and then marking it off – a sure way to secure the accuracy, but not to save room in a limited space'. This shows that the plants were drawn life-size, a tradition that was also upheld (and still is), in *Curtis's Botanical Magazine,* edited at that time by William Hooker in Glasgow. Wight sent the first of Rungiah's drawings to Hooker, who asked for the drawings in octavo, (200 to 250 mm tall) so they could be engraved more easily. Hooker published a selection of Rungiah's drawings in *Illustrations of Indian Botany* in parts, beginning around 1831, and in the early editions of *Hooker's Icones Plantarum* from 1837. Wight happened to see an early proof on a visit to Glasgow, and wrote 'how proud my friend Rungiah will be when he sees them'.

Wight's other artist, Govindoo, took over the production of illustrations in 1846, by which time Rungiah had been working for about 20 years. After Wight's retirement Govindoo continued to work for Hugh Cleghorn and then Richard Beddome, Wight's botanical successors in Madras.

When all these Indian paintings are viewed from a 21st-century perspective, their beauty is remarkable despite their original function as scientific illustrations. It has been said that many of them are flat, and do not have the three-dimensional quality of contemporary European flower paintings. This is probably partly because of the style of Mughal painting, but also perhaps because in the hot weather of India, the botanists took their plant presses into the field, and the plants were pressed as soon as they were gathered. On returning to camp, or to his studio, the artist would have been asked to draw the already flattened specimen, as arranged for the herbarium.

artists' signatures

Names or signatures of two artists from the Cresswell Collection and their English transliterations: Jack Joyenaday = Sheikh Zain al-Din; Ramdass = Ram Das.

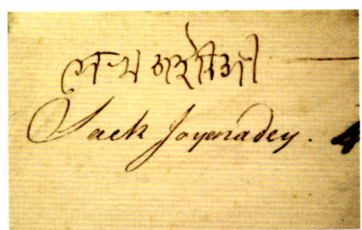

Later painters, and those who were definitely working from fresh specimens, could show ample perspective, for example, in the studies of *Magnolia campbellii*, painted for J.F. Cathcart in the 1840s.

Artists frequently had to create their own colours from local materials (plants and minerals), and could not buy artificial colours produced on an industrial scale, so the subtleties they managed to convey are the more remarkable. We can see from the blackening of many white flowers that lead white (lead carbonate) was often used, even from the late 18th century, by Lady Impey's artists. With the effects of damp and atmospheric sulphur, lead carbonate turns into lead sulphide, which is an unsightly black, though the discolouration can be reversed by oxidation using hydrogen peroxide.

Benjamin Heyne described the preparation of lead white, and used mercuric sulphide for red, and arsenic sulphide for yellow. Traditional colours were often used – burnt earths or rice for browns and black, turmeric for yellow, and extract of leaves for green; indigo for blue and *Butea* or *Hibiscus* flowers for red. Ground conch shell is used as a white base, and *Acacia catechu* gum as a binder. Rungiah and Govindoo, in particular, are recorded as 'mixing their own colours' and locally-sourced materials are still used by artists such as Mahaveer Swami (see page 207), who uses traditional techniques.

European paints (such as those sold by Reeves & Woodyer or Winsor & Newton) were imported into India but in 1837, in a letter to Hooker, Wight complained of the difficulty of getting a good supply of colours, and the lack of books on how to prepare paints. His concern at the time was for their use by the colourists of the lithographs destined for publication, so large quantities would have been required.

Smoothing or burnishing, a technique to improve the surface of the paper for fine work and to ensure binding of the colours, can be seen in paintings by Sheikh Zain al-Din, Bhawani Das and Ram Das. They also used Arabic gum to give extra sheen to some of the painted surfaces, particularly of leaves.

In the paintings shown here the artists names are given where they have been recorded. Though the majority of the paintings in the Cresswell family collection (see page 73) are unsigned, the signatures of the three artists appear on the back of some paintings in English and in Bengali script.

pitcher plant

Nepenthes ampullaria
(Nepenthaceae)

By Manu Lall, an artist from Patna, for Richard Parry in Sumatra, *c.* 1810.

This species is unusual in having a ring of small pitchers, unlike most species that have one large pitcher hanging at the tip of a leaf.

Himalayan fan palm
Trachycarpus martianus
(Arecaceae)

Probably by Vishnupersaud, for Nathaniel Wallich in Calcutta, *c.* 1825.

Found in Nepal, and closely related to the hardy Chinese fan palm, *Trachycarpus fortunei*, which in contrast has a very shaggy trunk, covered with fibrous leaf bases.

clubmoss
Huperzia squarrosa
(Lycopodiaceae)

By Manu Lall, for Richard Parry in Sumatra, *c.* 1810.

This clubmoss grows on trees in warm humid climates, hanging down from the branches of trees: it is also popular for growing in hanging baskets in the tropics or in a warm greenhouse.

vine

Stephania japonica var. *discolor* (Menispermaceae)

By Mogul-Ian, for Adam Freer, Behrampur, *c.* 1810.

A tropical climber, found from the Himalayas to Northern Australia. When illustrated without flowers, this was mistaken for a species of pepper, which has similar leaves.

→
melons

Cucumis spp. (Cucurbitaceae)

By Vishnupersaud, for John Royle, Saharanpur, *c.* 1828.

This is the original painting for the plate in Royle's *Illustrations of the Botany and Other Branches of the Natural History of the Himalayan Mountains, and of the Flora of Cashmere* vol. 2: t. 47 (1839). It shows two different species, *Cucumis pubescens* and *C. pseudocolocynthis*, both now considered to be forms of *C. melo* (melon), and *C. hardwickii,* now considered to be a form of *C. sativus* (cucumber).

sandpaper tree
Dillenia scabrella (Dilleniaceae)

By Gorachand, for Nathaniel Wallich in Calcutta, *c.* 1820.

This tree can reach to 12 m or so, and is found wild from Assam to Thailand and Vietnam. John Roxburgh introduced it from Chittagong to the Calcutta Botanic Garden in 1807; its flowers appear on the bare branches in early spring, and it is in leaf in the rainy season. The fleshy sepals, which are slightly acidic, are used in curries. This is the original painting for the plate in Wallich's *Plantae Asiaticae Rariores* 1: t. 22 (1830).

Kashmir sage
Phlomis cashmeriana (Lamiaceae)

By Luchman Singh, for John Royle, Saharanpur, *c.* 1828.

This perennial grows on dry slopes from Kashmir to Afghanistan, and forms large clumps, with many stems. This is the original painting for the plate in Royle's *Illustrations of the Botany and Other Branches of the Natural History of the Himalayan Mountains, and of the Flora of Cashmere.*

→ climber
Mucuna monosperma (Leguminosae)

By Rungiah, for Robert Wight probably in Negapatam, *c.* 1829.

A very robust, woody climber, found wild along rivers in the forests from India and Sri Lanka to Thailand. Wight reported that it is particularly common in the Northern Circars near Samulcottah (Samarlakota) in Andhra Pradesh. This is the original painting for the plate in William Hooker's *Botanical Miscellany* 2(6): 346, supplementary part t. xii (1831).

THE SCOTTISH SURGEON-BOTANISTS

IN THE CHAPTERS THAT FOLLOW, THE PLANT PAINTINGS ARE grouped under the botanists who commissioned them. It is remarkable that most of the botanists concerned, at least between 1770 and 1850, were trained as doctors, and began work as surgeons for the Company. At that time, botany was an important part of the medical course, especially as most drugs were still plant based, and the professors of botany were often influential in arousing the interest of their pupils in the study of plants, which would last through their later careers. The majority of those who served in India were Scottish, often the younger sons of small landowners, and educated at Edinburgh University. They began immediately after qualifying, as 'assistant surgeons' in the service of the Company.

A list of the major early botanists and their universities shows the dominance of Edinburgh in medical training at this time, and includes Patrick Russell (1750) who came to India via a posting in Aleppo; Adam Freer (1767) and William Roxburgh (1774); Francis Buchanan (afterwards Hamilton) (1783); Robert Wight (1818); Alexander Gibson (surgeon's diploma 1820); Hugh Falconer (1829) and Hugh Cleghorn (1841). Others who also graduated in medicine were Benjamin Heyne, a German Moravian missionary *c.* 1790, Nathaniel Wallich at Copenhagen University in 1821; William Griffith at University College, London; John Forbes Royle, in Munich, 1833; Joseph Dalton Hooker, Glasgow,1839 and John Ellerton Stocks, London, 1844.

The most influential of the teachers of botany in Edinburgh was John Hope, professor of botany and Regius keeper of the already century-old botanic garden from 1761 until 1786. His botanical courses were taught in the garden in the summer and in them he emphasised the importance of careful observation and fieldwork, using as examples plants in the garden. With his profusely illustrated lectures and commissioning of botanical artists he also impressed on his students

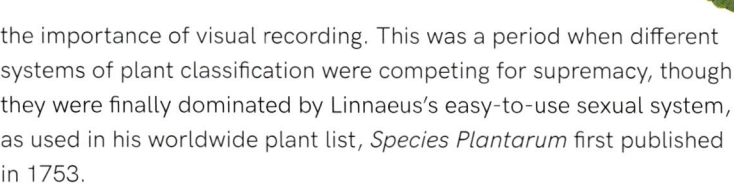

the importance of visual recording. This was a period when different systems of plant classification were competing for supremacy, though they were finally dominated by Linnaeus's easy-to-use sexual system, as used in his worldwide plant list, *Species Plantarum* first published in 1753.

Hope's successor, from 1786 until 1819, was Daniel Rutherford, better known as a chemist, one of the first to isolate nitrogen, but his botany lectures are said to have been popular and took place in the botanic garden at 8 o'clock in the morning. The next holder of the joint posts of professor and Regius keeper, from 1820 until 1845, was Robert Graham, who had previously held the botanical chair at Glasgow. At Glasgow, Graham was succeeded by William Jackson Hooker, who with his son Joseph Dalton Hooker made the study of the Indian flora a large part of their life's work, and at the same time built up a substantial part of the collections of paintings and herbarium specimens at the Royal Botanic Gardens, Kew.

Beginning with William Roxburgh, often called the 'father of Indian botany', who arrived in Madras in 1776, the different activities and careers of the young surgeons are described below. They usually began by being assistants to more senior doctors, ministering to the Company's staff, both Indian and European. The lucky ones were soon allowed to specialise in botany or be in charge of experimental gardens, and there were even a few specifically botanical posts where the study of local flora was an important aspect of the job.

Those who were less fortunate, such as Robert Wight, had to spend many years concentrating on medicine. Wight even had a short spell in charge of Tipu Sultan's cattle-breeding station in Mysore (Mysuru), which was set up to breed strong bullocks for transport.

henbane

Hyoscyamus niger (Solanaceae)

Artist unknown, for Adam Freer, Behrampur, *c.* 1810.

This painting of a common, poisonous weed is in an unusually primitive style, closer to that of a medieval Latin herbal than an Indian or European 18th-century illustration. Though extremely toxic, Henbane was used as a medicinal plant in ancient times, for pain relief, and as a sedative, but can also cause hallucinations.

mountain cassia

Senna montana (as *Cassia montana* (Leguminosae)

Artist unknown, for Benjamin Heyne in Madras, *c.* 1798.

This forms a large shrub or small tree, flowering in winter. It is found mainly in south India, growing in dry scrub in the hills. The bark and leaves are used against fevers and headache.

←
Himalayan monkshood
Aconitum ferox (Ranunculaceae)

Probably by Vishnupersaud, for John Royle, Saharanpur, *c.* 1828.

This very deadly plant, which grows at high altitudes in the Himalayas, was also illustrated by Vishnupersaud for Wallich, who gave a long account of it in *Plantae Asiaticae Rariores* t. 41 (1830), saying that it is the most 'deleterious vegetable poison of continental India'. The alternative European name of monkshood, wolfsbane, refers to its effect on dogs. In one experiment, two grains put into the jugular vein of a strong dog, produced death in three minutes. This agrees with its traditional use for anointing poison arrows, and the poison is almost as deadly when eaten.

woolly dyeing rosebay
Wrightia arborea (as *Nerium tomentosum*) (Apocynaceae)

Artist unknown, for William Roxburgh, Calcutta, *c.* 1800.

This tree is closely related to Oleander. The flowers smell of rotten fruit; the bark is used medicinally and for a yellow dye. The leaves of another species, *Wrightia tinctoria* yield a blue dye, which can be used as a substitute for indigo and the species is also used medicinally. Until recently this tree was known as *Wrightia tomentosa*.

vasaka or Malabar nut
Justicia adhatoda
(Acanthaceae)

Artist unknown, for William Roxburgh, Calcutta, *c.* 1800.

A tropical or subtropical shrub which grows wild from Pakistan to Malaya and South-East Asia, and is commonly cultivated elsewhere; the leaves and other parts of the plant contain the alkaloid vasicine, and are a well-known and popular remedy for colds, coughs, and asthma.

ashwagandha or Indian ginseng →
Withania somnifera
(as *Physalis somnifera*) (Solanaceae)

Probably by Rungiah, for Robert Wight in Madras, *c.* 1828.

A shrubby perennial with thick and fleshy roots which smell of horses; the flowers are small and green, the fruits bright red when ripe, enclosed in a papery husk. The powdered root is commonly used in Ayurvedic medicine, and was well-known to the ancients. It is now found all round the world, but probably originated in India.

pennywort
Hydrocotyle himalaica (Apiaceae)

Artist unknown, for John Cathcart in Darjeeling, *c.* 1850.

This is a creeping perennial, which grows on the banks of streams and in damp shady places in the hills at up to 2,450 m, common in the Himalaya from Nepal to southwest China, Burma and Hainan Is. The very similar *Centella asiatica*, which is widely used in traditional medicine, has reddish stems and peduncles much shorter than the leaves; it is found wild from Africa and the Caucasus to Japan and New Zealand. Some of the heads of flowers are unfinished, and show as white circles on the leaves.

→
hogweed
Tetrataenium nepalense (Apiaceae)

Artist unknown, for John Cathcart in Darjeeling, *c.* 1850.

A large herb found in the mountains from Nepal to Burma and western China, often growing along roads and in other disturbed ground, in pine and fir forest, to 4,000 m. The common name indicates that the flowers have a distinct smell of pigs.

Himalayan rhubarb

Rheum australe (as *R. emodi*) (Polygonaceae)

Artist unknown, for John Cathcart in Darjeeling, *c.* 1850.

This species grows at high altitude from Himachal Pradesh to Sikkim and Bhutan, and is very similar to the edible rhubarb, *R. rhabarbarum* which originates in northern China. Red stems and flowers, and rounded leaves are characteristic of *R. australe*. The young stems are a rich source of vitamin K. The roots are also used medicinally, especially to relieve constipation.

LADY IMPEY AND SHEIKH ZAIN AL-DIN IN CALCUTTA

LADY IMPEY ARRIVED IN CALCUTTA WITH HER HUSBAND Sir Elijah in autumn 1774. They took a large house, garden and park, with ample staff, and Lady Impey, who was young, (only 25 years old), intelligent and energetic, ran the establishment, including a menagerie of rare birds and animals, and her nine children, while her husband was acting as chief justice of the Supreme Court of Calcutta. They learnt Bengali and Urdu on the voyage to India, and on arrival started to learn Persian. Soon their house became a meeting place for the more intellectual members of Calcutta society, and they also became friends with Claude Martin and visited him in Lucknow.

At the same time Lady Impey and her husband made a valuable collection of natural history paintings, employing three artists, Sheikh Zain al-Din, Bhawani Das and Ram Das, who described themselves as 'natives of Patna', and may have been trained in the court of the Nawab of Bengal in Murshidabad and Patna. All three concentrated initially on bird paintings, often, in the Chinese tradition, accompanied by, or perching on a flowering branch. Many of Bhawani Das's fish paintings date from the end of the Impey's stay in India in 1783. After the death of Sir Elijah in 1809, the Impey's collection was sold in London, and the paintings dispersed.

After the departure of the Impeys in December 1783, the three artists continued to paint for English visitors and members of the Asiatic Society of Bengal, including the orientalist Sir William Jones (1746-1794), a noted lawyer, Persian scholar and linguist, one of the founders of the Society, who made a special study of the Sanskrit names of plants. Sir William certainly had flower paintings by Sheikh Zain al-Din in his collection, one of which is dated 1787. He became interested in botany during a period of sickness in 1784, when on his way to Benares. Many drawings by Indian artists, and by Lady Jones herself, are in the Royal Asiatic Society in London; he intended to publish a treatise on the plants of India, but died before it was completed.

THE CRESSWELL FAMILY COLLECTION

Work by the artists employed by Lady Impey has recently been found among a large number of plant and animal illustrations donated by the Cresswell family to the Royal Albert Memorial Museum & Art Gallery in Exeter, Devon. Seventy-eight paintings are of Indian plants in the style of the Calcutta botanical artists. Most are unsigned, without notes or indications of provenance, but a few have the artist's name on the back, both in Bengali and in English transliteration. Dr Nandini Chatterjee of the University of Exeter has read the names and confirmed that the artists are the same as those employed by Lady Impey. What appeared to be Jack (or Sack) Joyenadey, is a particularly strange Anglicisation. She writes that 'the Bengali version shows us that "Sack" is an Anglophone corruption of Sheikh, and Joyenadey is a corruption of the name Zain al-Din, which is pronounced in Arabic, Persian and Urdu as Zainuddin, but in Bengali as Joinuddi.' The two other artist's names, Ram Das and Bhawani Das, are less corrupted.

There is no documentation for the drawings' path from Calcutta to Exeter, but they may have come from the Creighton family. The most likely commissioner is Henry Creighton (1764–1807), a merchant who gave plants to the Calcutta Botanic Garden. Having arrived in Bengal in 1783, he became manager of an indigo factory. As an amateur antiquarian he pioneered the study of the ruins of Gaur; he died in 1807 and is buried beside Adam Freer in Behrampur. His son Robert entered the service of the EIC in 1814, married Emily Cheap in 1818, but died aged 30 leaving five children. Their second daughter Frances was born in 1821 and in 1840 went with her mother to England, settling in Kent. In 1843 she married the young curate there, Richard Cresswell, who moved to Devon, becoming eminent in the study of marine algae. Frances herself was a keen amateur botanist and would have treasured the paintings collected by her grandfather.

However, given the presence of various printed sheets of different Indian plants in the collection, for example a proof sheet of Royle's

Illustrations of Botany of the Himalayan Mountains with notes for the colourist (eventually published in 1835 in London), several uncoloured plates from Robert Wight's publications, a group of paintings of Malay fruits, and other miscellaneous illustrations, it seems that the collection was added to by later generations of the Cresswell family. Some of them practised as doctors in London, and were also interested in English wildflowers, of which they made paintings in the mid-19th century.

glory lily

Gloriosa superba (Colchicacaeae)

Artist unknown, possibly Sheikh Zain al-Din, *c.* 1800.

Gloriosa is a beautiful climbing or scrambling lily-like plant, found wild in grassy places, the stems growing in summer from an elongated tuberous root. The flowers are usually red with a wavy yellow edge, but can vary in colour from all yellow to all red. The shiny leaves have coiled tips which hang onto grass or shrubs. The whole plant is very poisonous, containing colchicine, which causes chromosome duplication. In southern India it is used to treat many ailments, notably for gout and worms, as a laxative or to produce abortion. Cresswell Collection: © Royal Albert Memorial Museum & Art Gallery, Exeter City Council.

The 'Creighton' paintings are beautifully drawn, fully coloured, in a simple, elegant two-dimensional style, typical of Mughal painters and less European than similar plants painted for General Hardwicke, now in the British Library. Most are of plants used in Ayurvedic medicine, and may have been chosen for their medicinal interest as well as their decorative value. They probably date from between 1784 and 1800, assuming that they were painted after Lady Impey had ceased to employ her three artists.

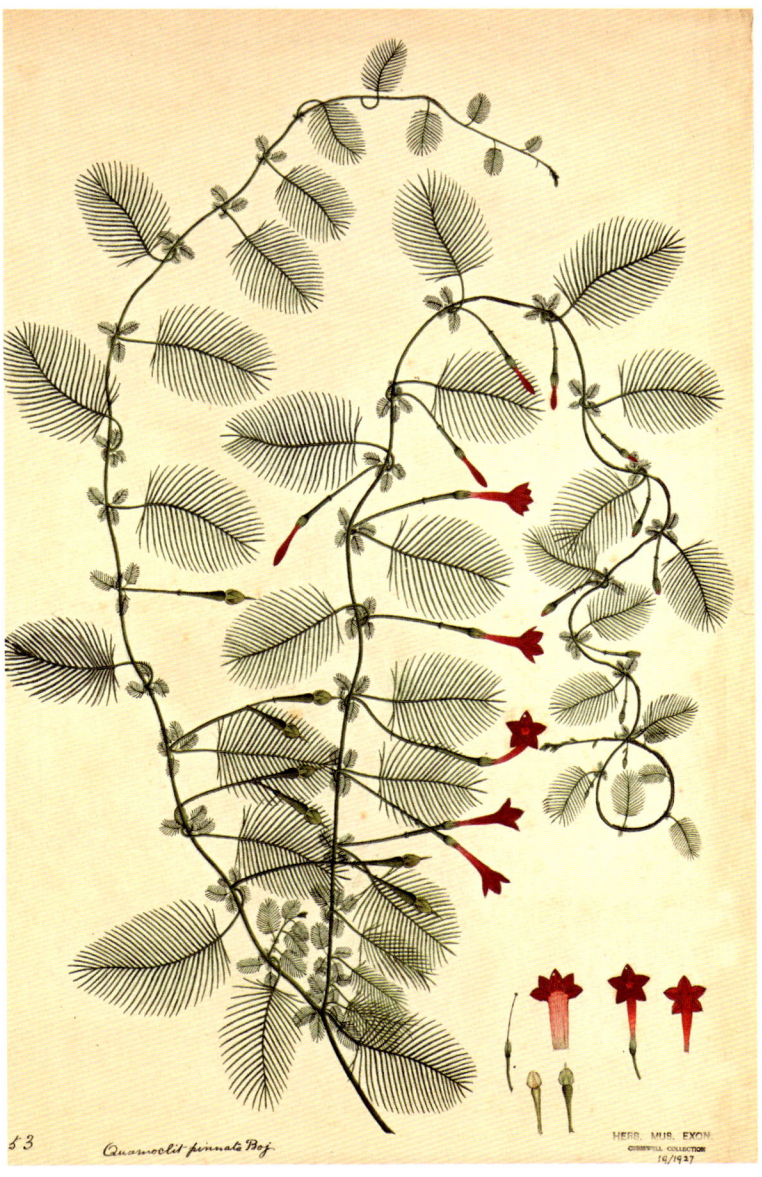

cardinal vine

Ipomoea quamoclit
(Convolvulaceae)

Artist unknown, possibly Sheikh Zain al-Din, *c.* 1800.

This beautiful climber is now found throughout the tropics, but probably originated in Mexico and South America. It is popular as an ornamental and easily grown from seed, planted in early summer; it requires warm, moist conditions, and then the stems can reach 3 m high and the plants flower well in early autumn. In India it is used medicinally to treat piles, and the black seeds are used as a purgative. Cresswell Collection: © Royal Albert Memorial Museum & Art Gallery, Exeter City Council.

musk mallow

Abelmoschus moschatus (Malvaceae)

Artist unknown, possibly Sheikh Zain al-Din, *c.* 1800.

This beautiful hibiscus-like herb is well-known in warm parts of India and China for its medicinal uses, and is related to Okra (*Abelmoschus esculentus*). The stems can reach 1.5 m tall; the flowers are around 15 cm across and the curved seeds are sweetly, musk-scented. Seeds, roots and leaves are used in herbal medicine. Cresswell Collection: © Royal Albert Memorial Museum & Art Gallery, Exeter City Council.

candle bush

Senna alata (often called *Cassia alata*) (Leguminosae)

By Sheikh Zain al-Din, *c.* 1800.

This is a large shrub to 4 m tall, now found in Africa and Asia, eastwards to Malaysia, though it probably originated in Mexico. It is the seedpods (not shown in the painting) that are winged, and give the plant its Latin name, and the English name refers to the upright, candle-like flower spikes. Bark, wood, leaves and seeds are all used medicinally; phenolic compounds from the pulverised leaves have been found to be anti-fungal, particularly against ringworm, and anti-bacterial helping the healing of skin. Like many species of *Senna*, it is also useful as a laxative. Cresswell Collection: © Royal Albert Memorial Museum & Art Gallery, Exeter City Council.

Indian almond

Terminalia catappa (Combretaceae)

By Bhawani Das, *c.* 1800.

Though no relation of the true almond (*Amygdalus*), this tall, evergreen tree has edible, almond-like oily fruits. It is often planted in coastal areas throughout the tropics, as it is tolerant of salt; the fruits float and are dispersed in the sea. The timber is good and of a rich reddish colour. The leaves can be used to feed silkworms. Both leaves and bark are rich in tannins and are used medicinally in many different cultures; they are thought to have potential for the treatment of some cancers and for the alleviation of sickle-cell anaemia, but other *Terminalia* species are more commonly used in Indian medicine. Cresswell Collection: © Royal Albert Memorial Museum & Art Gallery, Exeter City Council.

cat's whiskers

Cleome gynandra, formerly *Cleome pentaphylla* or *Gynandropsis pentaphylla* (Cleomaceae)

By Sheikh Zain al-Din, *c.* 1800.

This is an upright annual, often grown as a vegetable; it probably originated in Africa, but is now found throughout the tropics and subtropics, growing as a weed. It is the young shoots and leaves that are usually eaten, and they contain valuable vitamins and minerals. The flowers have an unusual structure: the petals are at the base of the flower, and an extension of the axis (called an androgynophore) has a whorl of long stamens and a further extension (a gynophore) ends in the ovary and style. Cresswell Collection: © Royal Albert Memorial Museum & Art Gallery, Exeter City Council.

WILLIAM ROXBURGH IN MADRAS AND CALCUTTA

BEFORE THE EARLY 17TH CENTURY, THE CITY OF MADRAS, on the Coromandel Coast, was an unimportant town, but was transformed into a trading station for the then still small EIC. The Company's earlier base in India was at Surat, north of Bombay but, in days when ships had to come round the Cape of Good Hope, this was a long way from the main trade route to China. In 1644 the Company built Fort St George and by establishing good relations with the local ruler was allowed to trade without customs dues. In the 1680s the Qing court in China eased its restrictions on foreign trade, and Indian ports, especially Madras and Calcutta, became important staging posts on the voyage from China to Europe, as well as entry points of Chinese goods for India.

Over the next 70 years Madras expanded into a thriving port and commercial centre, in spite of not having a sheltered harbour or major river mouth, in contrast to the cities of Calcutta or Dacca. Large trading ships had to anchor offshore and passengers and goods were ferried ashore in 'massulah' boats, heavy but flexible gig-style clinker-built vessels, propelled by oars and poles, which could come ashore or be launched through the surf. Contemporary accounts record that passengers often suffered a soaking.

The surgeon and botanist William Roxburgh first arrived in Madras in July 1774, as surgeon's mate on a Company ship, bound for Calcutta. He visited again in June 1775, after a journey of 144 days from London, before reaching Macau and Canton in October 1775. Here Roxburgh jumped ship, (forfeiting his pay for the voyage), and travelled back to India in 1776, again to Madras, where he managed to get himself appointed as an assistant surgeon at the General Hospital close to Fort St George in May 1776, which had been set up by Elihu Yale in the 1680s.

In 1776 Roxburgh was aged 25, having been born in Craigie, Ayrshire, a small rural village south of Glasgow, where his father probably

worked on the local estate. As a clever, poor boy he was sent to study in Edinburgh, entering the course in anatomy and surgery.

In Madras, in addition to his medical work in the hospital, Roxburgh made detailed meteorological records, which resulted in his first scientific publications. His next work was on indigo, and then on various other plants, studying both their botany and their medicinal uses. He sent plant specimens and seeds to Sir Joseph Banks, president of the Royal Society in London, and became friends with the botanist Johann König, who had been a pupil of Linnaeus and travelled to India as surgeon to the Danish colony of Tranquebar. König transferred to the employment of the Nawab of Arcot, and in 1778 was appointed as the official naturalist on the Madras Establishment of the Company.

From his base at Fort St George Roxburgh explored inland and in 1781 he was appointed surgeon at Nagore, further south on the Coromandel Coast, from where he was evicted by Haider Ali, Sultan of Mysore. His next move was to the north of Madras, in coastal Andhra, to the army camp at Samulcotta, near Coringa (Korangi). All this time Roxburgh was accumulating plant specimens, flower paintings and books. But in May 1787 disaster struck: a cyclone devastated much of the district near Coringa, and he lost his house and all his possessions, narrowly escaping to higher ground with his family. The sea reached 12 or 13 feet above its usual level, and around 15,000 people were said to have drowned. As he wrote: 'all we saved was ourselves, and just what we had on our backs. I had not even time to carry off Mrs R's jewels; what I regret most was a most valuable Botanical library, all my Manuscripts, Drawings, preserved specimens of plants &c which I had been collecting since I came to India.'

Through the help of friends, Roxburgh built up his collection again, and continued in various medical posts. König died in 1785, with Roxburgh at his bedside, and was followed as Company naturalist by

Patrick Russell, who had been in India since 1771, following a posting to Aleppo. He is best known as a herpetologist and ichthyologist, and as the author of *An account of Indian serpents*, published in 1796. Russell also had a collection of plant drawings, now in the Natural History Museum in London, and collected a large herbarium that he presented to his *alma mater*, Edinburgh University, and still survives at Royal Botanic Garden Edinburgh.

Russell retired from India in 1789, and, on his recommendation, Roxburgh was appointed his successor, with the title of company botanist on the Madras Coast. This included 'medicinal applications', as well as 'arts and manufactures', presumably from plant-based products. Thus in 1791, Roxburgh sent a paper to London on the lac insect, and in 1793, 'an account of a new species of *Nerium*, with the process of extracting, from its Leaves, a very beautiful Indigo'. This was called *Nerium tinctorium* by Roxburgh, but is now known as *Wrightia tinctoria*, a close relative of the oleander.

Roxburgh continued in the Madras area until 1793, collecting and studying plants, and developing crops that would be grown for profit and others that could feed the local population in times of famine, notably the food shortages that lasted from 1790 until 1792. Though contrary to Company policy, which did not allow non-Indians to own or rent land, Roxburgh obtained a five-year lease on land to farm on his own account. The exception was probably made because of Roxburgh's scientific experiments for the improvement of agriculture and he experimented with new or improved crops, particularly mulberry trees, sugar and indigo. He studied 26 different species for fibre, including the broom-like *Crotalaria juncea*, and local strains of hemp, flax, and several *Hibiscus* species including *H. cannabinus*. Both species of jute, (*Corchorus olitorius* and *C. capsularis*), traditional Indian crops, were first exported to Dundee in Scotland in around 1800.

By the time his lease came up for renewal, Roxburgh had obtained the job of superintendent of the Calcutta Botanic Garden, which he held between 1793 and 1813: here he continued his experimental work, and supervised the growing and dissemination of thousands of useful plants and tree seedlings all over eastern India.

Roxburgh's great illustrated botanical work is *Plants of the Coast of Coromandel*, published in London between 1795 and 1819. Duplicates of the 900 drawings commissioned by Roxburgh during his time in the Madras area were sent to the Company headquarters in London 'as a gift', and Roxburgh was at pains to point out that he had paid for them out of his own pocket. At the instigation of Patrick Russell, 300 of these were chosen and published under the direction of Sir Joseph Banks and his librarians, especially Jonas Dryander. The drawings were engraved and hand-coloured and, with accompanying descriptions, were published in groups of 25 to be gathered into three volumes. Unfortunately, we do not know the names of the artists, but there is a suggestion that there was one main artist, who accompanied Roxburgh to Calcutta. The main theme of Roxburgh's plant paintings from Madras is economic plants, whether used medicinally, as dyes or for fibre; plants used as food for silk moths or other commercially useful insects were also considered important.

cup-and-saucer plant

Holmskioldia sanguinea
(Lamiaceae)

Artist unknown, for William Roxburgh in Madras, *c.* 1790.

A beautiful shrub, found wild in northern India and Burma, named after Johan Holmskiold (1731-93), a Danish botanist and mycologist. Holmskiold was also secretary to the Dowager Queen Juliana Maria and a director of the Royal Danish Porcelain Factory, at the time that it began to use copies of illustrations from *Flora Danica* to decorate a service as a gift to Catherine the Great in Russia. The unusual flowers of *Holmskioldia* are made up of a red saucer-shaped calyx and narrow curved tubular flowers.

sohdanei

Garcinia pedunculata (Clusiaceae)

Artist unknown. for William Roxburgh in Madras, *c.* 1790.

Garcinia is a large genus of around 400 species of trees and shrubs, found mainly in tropical eastern Asia. The mangosteen, *G. mangostana*, is a popular fruit; the species illustrated here, *G. pedunculata*, has edible fruit, used in cooking in Assam, and is also potentially helpful against atherosclerosis. *G. cambogia* is used in curry, and commonly sold as a slimming aid. Camboge yellow is usually extracted from a different Indian species, *G. xanthochymus*.

→

amaltas

Cassia fistula (Leguminosae)

Artist unknown, for William Roxburgh in Madras, *c.* 1790.

This is one of the most beautiful tropical trees, also called golden shower or Indian laburnum, and is the state flower of Kerala. It is commonly planted throughout India, especially in dry areas. Trees can reach 20 m tall, and the hanging chains of flowers, produced in late spring, can be 40 cm long. The pulp in the fresh pods is used medicinally as a powerful purgative.

cashew nut

Anacardium occidentale (Anacardiaceae)

Artist unknown, for William Roxburgh in Madras, *c.* 1790.

Though best known for its nuts, this tropical American tree, long cultivated in India, has many other uses. The edible curved nuts are held in a hard acrid shell, and hang below the pear-shaped stalk, the cashew-apple which can be used to make a drink or liqueur. The shells contain a liquid used to strengthen plastics. The stems are the source of a valuable resin or varnish, acajou gum.

musk melon →

Cucumis melo (Cucurbitaceae)

Artist unknown, for William Roxburgh in Madras, *c.* 1790.

This painting shows a wild form of the musk melon, which has been used to develop edible varieties such as the cantaloupe and honeydew melon. It is probably a native of Africa, but brought to India in ancient times and grown for its edible seeds.

amaranth

Amaranthus hypochondriacus (*A. hybridus* var. *erythrostachys*) (Amaranthaceae)

Artist unknown, for William Roxburgh in Madras, *c.* 1790.

This red amaranth is commonly grown in India. The whole plant is edible, and can be grown like spinach and harvested when young; the seeds are also edible; this particular variety was selected and cultivated in central America in *c.* 4000 BCE.

cinnamon

Cinnamomum verum (*Laurus cinnamomum*) (Lauraceae)

Artist unknown, for William Roxburgh in Madras, *c.* 1790.

This tree is the source of the spice cinnamon, which is found in the dried aromatic bark; it is wild in south-west India and Sri Lanka, and usually cultivated as a coppiced shrub; the two-year old shoots are cut and the inner bark removed while still green, before drying.

elephant foot yam
Amorphophallus paeoniifolius often called
A. campanulatus (Araceae)

Artist unknown, for William Roxburgh in Madras, *c.* 1790.

Amorphophallus have large edible tubers, which are a valuable source of starch. They are commonly grown in Kerala, and taste like a rather grainy, nutty potato. The titan arum, *A. titanum* from Sumatra is grown as a crowd-puller in botanic gardens such as Kew; its flower (strictly an inflorescence), the biggest in the world, is particularly vast and stinking and its huge corm can weigh 50 kg, producing a single leaf which can be 4.5 m tall. In this species the leaf is only around 2 m tall, and the flower has a soft purplish frilly spathe around a purple bulbous folded spadix.

Indian coral tree

Erythrina variegata (Leguminosae)

Artist unknown, for William Roxburgh in Madras, *c.* 1790.

Erythrinas are stiff trees or shrubs with spikes of bright red flowers, usually pollinated by various nectar-feeding birds. In this species, which can form a large tree, the whole flowering shoot is bent sideways, so that the stem forms a perch, and all the stamens point towards the bird's head. Roxburgh's artist has carefully drawn the floral details, the seed and the leaf with glands near the base of the leaflets.

rice
Oryza sativa (Poaceae)

Artist unknown, for William Roxburgh in Madras, *c.* 1790.

This is an elegant example of cultivated rice, with details of the rootstock and of the flowers, each with six yellow stamens and two purple feathery styles.

→

sieva or lima bean
Phaseolus lunatus (Leguminosae)

Artist unknown, for William Roxburgh in Madras, *c.* 1790.

This bean is an ancient cultigen from Peru and central America and the wild forms are still found in Guatemala and in northern Peru: archaeological remains of cultivated Lima beans have been found near Paracas in Peru dating from around 3800 BCE, and the smaller Sieva beans have been recorded in Mexico from around 100 CE. Both forms were probably introduced into India in the 16th century. The white flowered and white seeded variety is shown here, with beans of a brown-seeded and black and white veined form.

turmeric or haldi
Curcuma longa (Zingiberaceae)

Artist unknown, for William Roxburgh in Madras, *c.* 1790.

Turmeric is now popular as a 'wonder drug' for arthritis and joint pain, but has a long history of cultivation in India, both as a medicinal plant and as a spice giving it a golden yellow colour. It is also used as a yellow dye, cheaper but less colourfast than saffron.

Curcuma euchroma, formerly known as *Curcuma zerumbet* (Zingiberaceae)

Artist unknown, for William Roxburgh in Madras, *c.* 1790.

This is the drawing on which was based plate 201 of Roxburgh's *Plants of the Coast of Coromandel* (1819). It is found wild in various parts of India, and is used medicinally for many different ailments.

Argyreia cymosa, formerly known as *Lettsomia cymosa* (Convolvulaceae)

Artist unknown, for William Roxburgh in Madras, *c.* 1790.

This attractive climber was initially named as a convolvulus, but Roxburgh later coined the name *Lettsomia* for this group, named after John Coakley Lettsom (1744–1815), a renowned Quaker, physician, entomologist and botanist, who wrote a dissertation on the tea tree.

→

Indian traveller's joy

Clematis gouriana (Ranunculaceae)

Artist unknown, for William Roxburgh in Madras, *c.* 1790.

This is a very common climber, found throughout India, scrambling over bushes and small trees. This is an example of the highly accomplished work of Roxburgh's artist, making beautiful and scientifically accurate designs from the apparently chaotic leaves and stem of climbing plants.

BENJAMIN HEYNE: A NATURALIST IN MADRAS

WILLIAM ROXBURGH'S SUCCESSOR AS MADRAS NATURALIST WAS Benjamin Heyne, a Moravian missionary who was born in Germany in 1770 and arrived in 1791 at the Danish settlement at Tranquebar, south of Madras. He soon became friendly with Roxburgh and other doctors interested in natural history. After Roxburgh moved to Calcutta, Heyne continued to commission botanical drawings, probably using artists trained by Roxburgh, as well as making copies of paintings in Roxburgh's collection.

In his journal for July 1798, Heyne described how he organised the production of so many paintings while in camp. 'As Plants were daily brought in, I ordered the painter to draw only the outline with Indian Ink, and colour only one flower, fruit and leaf; by doing which I get a great many plants drawn.'

Completion of the colouring was carried out later, doubtless when installed in a more secure base. Heyne remained based in Madras until around 1802, when he supervised the move of Roxburgh's Samulcotta plants to a botanic garden in Bangalore, a post he held until 1808. Heyne is said to have given many of his paintings to the second Lord Clive while he was governor of Madras, and several volumes of Heyne's paintings are at the Royal Botanic Gardens, Kew, having been bought at Christie's auction house in 1965.

Heyne's paintings are simplified versions of Roxburgh's commissioned works rather than copies. They are clear and formally drawn, smaller than life-size, with a double ruled border. Some are named, some numbered, but to what list the numbers refer is not known.

phanera

Cheniella corymbosa also known as *Bauhinia corymbosa* (Leguminosae)

Artist unknown, for Benjamin Heyne in Madras, *c.* 1800.

This is a subtropical climber, popularly grown in gardens around the world, probably originating in China. The two-lobed leaves are typical of a *Bauhinia*.

bitter snake gourd

Trichosanthes tricuspidata, formerly known as *T. bracteata* (Cucurbitaceae)

Artist unknown, for Benjamin Heyne in Madras, *c.* 1800.

Trichosanthes are climbing gourds with solitary female flowers, and several male flowers in a raceme, as is shown here: the white petals have beautifully fringed margins, and the round fruits are bright red when ripe, with large dark seeds. Most species are poisonous, but used in Indian and Chinese traditional medicine.

climbing gourd

Momordica cymbalaria (Cucurbitaceae)

Artist unknown, for Benjamin Heyne in Madras, *c.* 1800.

This tuberous climbing gourd is found mainly in southern India, south to Tamil Nadu, and in eastern Africa; it has long been used medicinally, so it has been the subject of recent studies mainly for its antioxidant properties. The stems can reach 5 m long: the fruits are cylindrical, around 6 cm long and ridged when ripe. It is related to the bitter cucumber or bitter gourd, *M. charantia*.

ADAM FREER AND CHUNILALL IN BENGAL

ADAM FREER (1747–1811) WAS ANOTHER OF THE BOTANIST-physicians educated in Edinburgh, and, like Roxburgh and Buchanan, was taught botany by Dr John Hope. The details of his life in India are not well documented, but his collection of 382 Indian plant drawings, now at the Royal Botanic Gardens, Kew, show that he was a keen botanist. While still at Edinburgh, Freer made for Hope a catalogue of plants around the city arranged by flowering time (and doubtless originally accompanied by a herbarium). Freer graduated in 1767 and in around 1772 succeeded Patrick Russell as physician to the Levant Company in Aleppo. Here he continued to collect plant and animal specimens for Russell, who was revising his brother Alexander's *Natural History of Aleppo*. He also sent dried plants to Hope, one of the few elements of Hope's collection to survive in the Royal Botanic Garden Edinburgh's herbarium.

Freer followed Russell to India in 1781, travelling via Baghdad and Basra, and seems to have been based near Calcutta. He accompanied Kirkpatrick's expedition to Nepal in 1793, as surgeon, but the plants collected, if any, were not recorded. It seems, however, that he and others on the expedition were presented with a young elephant! Freer's interest in Bengali herbal medicine can be seen in one of his

few published papers, in 1801, on curing ringworm by vinegar in which bark, roots or flowers of *Senna sophera* have been steeped; this is still a popular herbal and homeopathic cure for several skin diseases.

From 1809 Freer was superintending surgeon for the Company at Behrampur, and he died there in 1811. Curiously, he is buried in the same cemetery as Henry Creighton, so they might well have known each other and discussed botanical painting. Freer sent his two young children, whose mother was Indian, back to Scotland, to the care of his brother, a medical professor in Glasgow who would later become a colleague of William Hooker.

The Freer collection of plant drawings is very varied in style and mostly undated, but with a substantial group dated 1809 or 1810. Most are of common vegetables, garden or paddy-field weeds, semi-wild trees and shrubs. Many are inscribed with the artist's name: Mogul-Ian, Chunilall, Bearilall, Brijlall and Sablall. The style of many of the paintings is simple and formal, similar to that seen in some late Medieval herbals, with an emphasis on design rather than naturalness. Chunilall also painted flowers for the MacGregor of MacGregor who was auditor general in Bengal at the end of the 18th century.

lemon

Citrus × *limon* (Rutaceae)

Artist unknown, for Adam Freer in Behrampur, *c.* 1810.

Lemons have been grown for thousands of years, and are thought to have originated as crosses between the citron *(C. medica)* and the orange *(C. × aurantium)*, possibly in Assam or northern Burma. They were grown in Europe in late Roman times, and used mainly for medicine, being very rich in vitamin C.

pomegranate

Punica granatum (Lythraceae)

Artist unknown, for Adam Freer in Behrampur, *c.* 1810.

The pomegranate is found wild across the warmer parts of Asia, from the western Himalaya to southeastern Europe, often growing as a shrub or small tree on cliffs by springs and water seepages. It has long been valued as a delicious and healthy fruit, ripening in late summer and autumn. The seeds have been found in Bronze Age Jericho (*c.* 1500 BCE); they are surrounded by a fleshy, juicy, pinkish pulp; the juice contains valuable antioxidants. The dried seeds with dark red pulp are known as anardana, and used in curries.

toon or Indian mahogany
Toona hexandra also called *Cedrela toona* (Meliaceae)

Probably by Samlall for Adam Freer in Behrampur, *c.* 1810.

Toona forms large trees to around 25 m in subtropical forests from Afghanistan and India south to eastern Australia. It belongs to the same family as American mahogany (*Swietenia*) and its timber is also valuable as well as being highly scented; it is used for furniture and musical instruments. Here the artist has drawn a highly stylised branch, using the leaves to form a background for the small white flowers.

←
kanak champa
Pterospermum acerifolium (Malvaceae)

By Brijlall, for Adam Freer in Behrampur in 1809.

This tree is wild in subtropical forests in northern India and is often planted for shade. It can reach 30 m in height and produces very hard and durable timber; the flowers are white, fragrant and open at night, and are sometimes collected for use as a disinfectant. In this painting the artist has used lead white for the pure white petals; it has absorbed sulphur from the air over time, to become black lead sulphide. This process can be reversed by treatment with hydrogen peroxide.

rue
Ruta graveolens (Rutaceae)

By Bearilall, for Adam Freer in Behrampur in 1809.

The common herb rue is native of the Mediterranean area, but is grown in the drier parts of India, as a flavouring and medicinal plant. It is very poisonous and was often used to produce abortion. In many people, the juice combined with exposure to sunlight causes inflammation and peeling of the skin.

coriander
Coriandrum sativum (Apiaceae)

Artist unknown, for Adam Freer in Behrampur, *c.* 1810.

Coriander originates from the eastern Mediterranean, and has long been cultivated as a flavouring; its trade is mentioned in Linear B tablets from Knossos in Crete, which date from around 1200 BCE; roots, leaves and seeds are all commonly used today. Roasted and ground seeds are an important constituent of curry powder.

CLAUDE MARTIN AND THE LUCKNOW ARTISTS

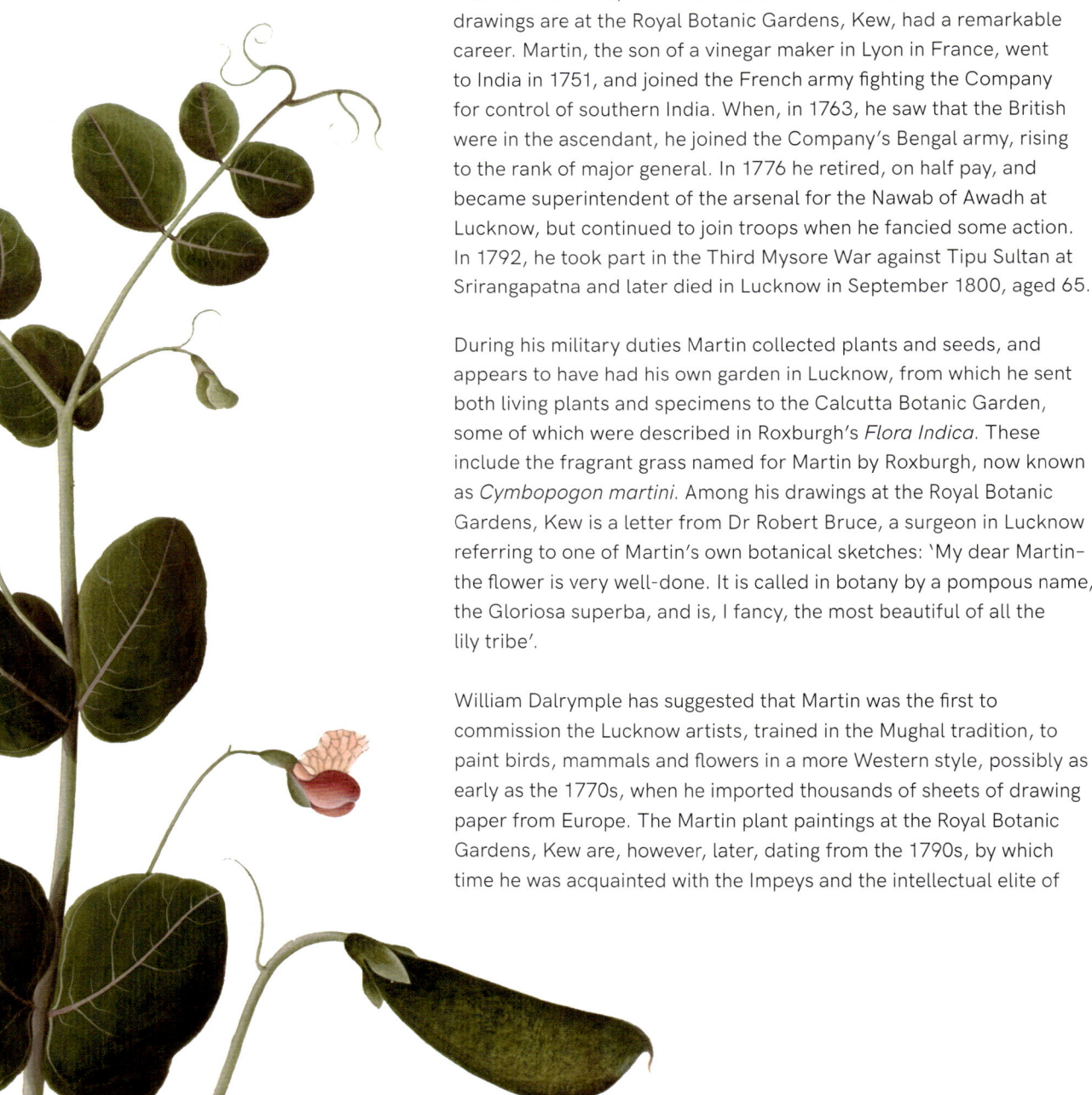

CLAUDE MARTIN, WHOSE COLLECTION OF ALMOST 600 PLANT drawings are at the Royal Botanic Gardens, Kew, had a remarkable career. Martin, the son of a vinegar maker in Lyon in France, went to India in 1751, and joined the French army fighting the Company for control of southern India. When, in 1763, he saw that the British were in the ascendant, he joined the Company's Bengal army, rising to the rank of major general. In 1776 he retired, on half pay, and became superintendent of the arsenal for the Nawab of Awadh at Lucknow, but continued to join troops when he fancied some action. In 1792, he took part in the Third Mysore War against Tipu Sultan at Srirangapatna and later died in Lucknow in September 1800, aged 65.

During his military duties Martin collected plants and seeds, and appears to have had his own garden in Lucknow, from which he sent both living plants and specimens to the Calcutta Botanic Garden, some of which were described in Roxburgh's *Flora Indica*. These include the fragrant grass named for Martin by Roxburgh, now known as *Cymbopogon martini*. Among his drawings at the Royal Botanic Gardens, Kew is a letter from Dr Robert Bruce, a surgeon in Lucknow referring to one of Martin's own botanical sketches: 'My dear Martin– the flower is very well-done. It is called in botany by a pompous name, the Gloriosa superba, and is, I fancy, the most beautiful of all the lily tribe'.

William Dalrymple has suggested that Martin was the first to commission the Lucknow artists, trained in the Mughal tradition, to paint birds, mammals and flowers in a more Western style, possibly as early as the 1770s, when he imported thousands of sheets of drawing paper from Europe. The Martin plant paintings at the Royal Botanic Gardens, Kew are, however, later, dating from the 1790s, by which time he was acquainted with the Impeys and the intellectual elite of

Calcutta. Apart from collecting plants and animals, Martin was a lavish patron of arts and crafts of all kinds. There are several paintings of him by Zoffany, dating from around 1786, including one of his favourite mistress, Boulone, clad in trousers and boots and wielding a long fishing rod, with Martin's adopted son James looking on.

Martin's collection of plant and animal drawings was given to, or purchased by, Sir Gore Ouseley, who also served the Nawab of Awadh in Lucknow during the time Martin was living there. Ouseley left the drawings to his son, a professor of music at Oxford, and they were eventually purchased for the Royal Botanic Gardens, Kew, along with a number of paintings of Caucasian plants made for Ouseley when he was in Tabriz negotiating peace treaties between Persia, England and Russia, in around 1812.

Martin's chief distinction is the huge fortune he made for himself, and the philanthropic way he arranged for it to be spent after his death. He instructed that the bulk of his fortune be used to set up schools in India and in France. There are now two La Martinière colleges in Kolkata and two in Lucknow, as well as three in Lyon; the Lucknow boys' college is housed in the particularly magnificent building named Constantia, designed by Martin as his grand residence and described by Dalrymple as 'part Enlightenment mansion, part Nawabi fantasy, and part Gothic colonial barracks.'

Martin's plant drawings, by artists whose names are sadly unrecorded, are in diverse styles, some simple, without perspective, others in a more western European style. The subjects are from the plains and gardens of northern India, with a large proportion of herbal and cultivated plants.

cannabis, ganja

Cannabis sativa (Cannabaceae)

Artist unknown, for Claude Martin in Lucknow, *c.* 1790.

Cannabis has been grown in India for thousands of years, and different parts are eaten as well as smoked. It is valued for its therapeutic properties, but its adverse effects on mind and body were recognised in the ancient texts.

←
chrysanthemum

Chrysanthemum × morifolium (Asteraceae)

Artist unknown, for Claude Martin in Lucknow, *c.* 1795.

Chrysanthemums, now such popular flowers all over the world, originated in China. They were grown in gardens there from the 5th century BCE, and transported to Europe in the late 18th century, first to France and reaching England almost in the same year as this one was painted. This painting of two varieties shows that they were already established in India by the beginning of the 19th century.

garden peas
Pisum sativum (Leguminosae)

Artist unknown, for Claude Martin in Lucknow, *c.* 1790.

Shown here are two varieties of garden pea, found wild in the Mediterranean region east to Afghanistan, and long cultivated (since 7000 BCE), and found in ancient archaeological sites such as Jericho and Troy. Peas, lentils and green gram (mung beans) were grown in the Indus valley in around 3000 BCE. The early pea varieties all had bi-coloured flowers, as here. These two paintings of peas are very different in style. The illustration on the left is elegant and artistic, stylised and simplified, with unnaturally round leaves and stipules. The one on the right is European in style, more realistic, with folded leaves, a curved stem and carefully copied tendrils.

CLAUDE MARTIN & THE LUCKNOW ARTISTS

peepal tree, bohdi or bo tree
Ficus religiosa (Moraceae)

Artist unknown, for Claude Martin in Lucknow, *c.* 1790.

This is the famous fig tree under which the Buddha attained enlightenment, and is sacred to Hindus and Jains, as well as to Buddhists. Ancient trees can grow to 30 m in height and are often very wide. The leaves have a long thin stalk and a characteristic long pointed tip, known as a drip tip, which make heavy rain drain off freely. Like the leaves of aspens, they also move in the slightest breeze. The fruits are small, about 15 mm in diameter, purple when ripe. The peepal tree has many traditional medicinal uses, from asthma to diabetes, gastric and genito-urinary problems: the bark is the most important part of the tree, but leaves, latex, fruits and seeds are also used. The latex in particular is valuable as a fungicide.

FRANCIS BUCHANAN–HAMILTON AND HALUDAR IN CALCUTTA

DR FRANCIS BUCHANAN (1762–1829), WHO LATER TOOK THE name of Hamilton when he inherited his mother's estate in Scotland, was born near Glasgow and studied medicine in Edinburgh, including botany under Dr John Hope. Buchanan joined the Bengal Medical Service in 1794 and soon became friendly with William Roxburgh (see pages 80 and 126). Buchanan's main work was to make surveys of the natural resources of parts of India, including the botany, zoology, minerals and languages. He visited Burma in 1795, Chittagong (now in Bangladesh) in 1798, and in 1800–1801 was commissioned by Wellesley to undertake a major survey of Mysore after the defeat of Tipu Sultan. The botanical drawings from the Mysore survey, possibly by the Calcutta artist Haludar, are at the Linnean Society of London.

A remarkable story, recorded by Henry Noltie (1999), concerns a book of notes taken by Buchanan from Hope's botanical lectures in 1780: 'On his first voyage to the East in 1785, Buchanan lent the notes to his shipmate Alexander Boswell. Boswell, who failed to return the notes, lost them in 1790 during a military encounter at Satimangala where they fell into the hands of Tipu Sultan of Mysore, who had them rebound. At the siege of Seringapatam in 1800 they were found in Tipu's library by a Major Ogg, who returned them to Buchanan.'

Buchanan was also the first to undertake substantial botanical work in Nepal, based in the Kathmandu valley in 1802 and 1803 accompanied, as usual, by an artist. From 1803 to 1805 he was

surgeon on Wellesley's staff, which included supervising the making of zoological drawings at the menagerie at Barrackpore. Between 1807 and 1814 he ended his Indian career with a major survey of Bengal, the botanical drawings for which have recently been discovered at the Royal Botanic Gardens, Kew. At the same time, he was making a study of the fishes of the Ganges and its tributaries, which he wrote up in retirement and published in 1822.

In the very last month before his retirement to Scotland in 1815, Buchanan finally became superintendent of the Calcutta Botanic Garden, a post he had long desired, but which Roxburgh held on to for far longer than he should have. Buchanan was forced to leave his collection of paintings of plants, birds and animals from the Bengal Survey in Calcutta, but the botanical ones must eventually have been sent back to the Company's library in London and reached the Royal Botanic Gardens, Kew in 1879 when the Company museum was finally dispersed.

In his scholarly and active retirement in Scotland, Buchanan, by this time called Francis Hamilton, undertook a major project to identify the plants illustrated in van Rheede's *Hortus Indicus Malabaricus*. The resulting papers were read at 31 meetings of the Linnean Society in London until 1852, long after their author's death, but only those devoted to the first four volumes of van Rheede's work were ever published.

orchid

Dendrobium moschatum
(Orchidaceae)

Artist unknown, for Francis Buchanan-Hamilton, *c.* 1795.

The annotation 'From Pegu' suggests that this plant may have been collected near Pegu in Burma, but grown in a botanical garden in India, though it is also found in many areas from northern India to northern Thailand. This illustration is the type of the species, described in the *Account of an Embassy to the Kingdom of Ava*, sent by the governor-general of India, in the year 1795, published in 1800.

→
orchid

Ascocentrum ampullaceum
(Orchidaceae)

Artist unknown, for Francis Buchanan-Hamilton in Bengal, *c.* 1810.

This miniature epiphytic orchid is closely related to *Vanda*, and was originally described by Roxburgh in 1832 in the genus *Aerides*. It is found wild in evergreen forest from Nepal, Bhutan and India east to Thailand and southern Yunnan.

Indian almond, stinky sterculia

Sterculia foetida (Malvaceae)

Artist unknown, for Francis Buchanan-Hamilton in Bengal, c. 1810.

This *Sterculia* forms a tall tree with buttressed roots, to more than 30 m, with large, deeply divided leaves and masses of small red-brown and green flowers smelling of bad meat, around 12 mm across, the male and female on separate trees. It flowers in spring as the leaves open, and nearly a year later has red capsules containing many seeds, which may be roasted and eaten. It is found wild from tropical Africa and southern India to northern Australia. This painting shows a branch with female flowers.

pipewort
Eriocaulon sexangulare (Eriocaulaceae)

Artist unknown, for Francis Buchanan-Hamilton in Bengal, *c.* 1810.

Pipewort is usually a small aquatic plant, which grows in shallow water with the leaves submerged and the flower stems reaching up to the surface. There are around 400 species, with a remarkable wild distribution, mainly in the tropics, but with *E. aquaticum* found in the Hebrides in northern Scotland and Connemara in Ireland, as well as eastern North America. The species shown here is found from India to China and Japan, growing mainly in flooded rice paddies, as well as in Africa and Madagascar.

→
elephant yam
Amorphophallus bulbifer (Araceae)

Artist unknown, for Francis Buchanan-Hamilton in Bengal, *c.* 1809.

This yam is found in subtropical forests in northern India east to Burma. The flowering stem emerges in early summer, before the leaf, and reaches around 35 cm in height. The leaf of this species only reaches around 1 m and is divided into 12 or more lanceolate lobes, with small bulbils formed among the leaflets.

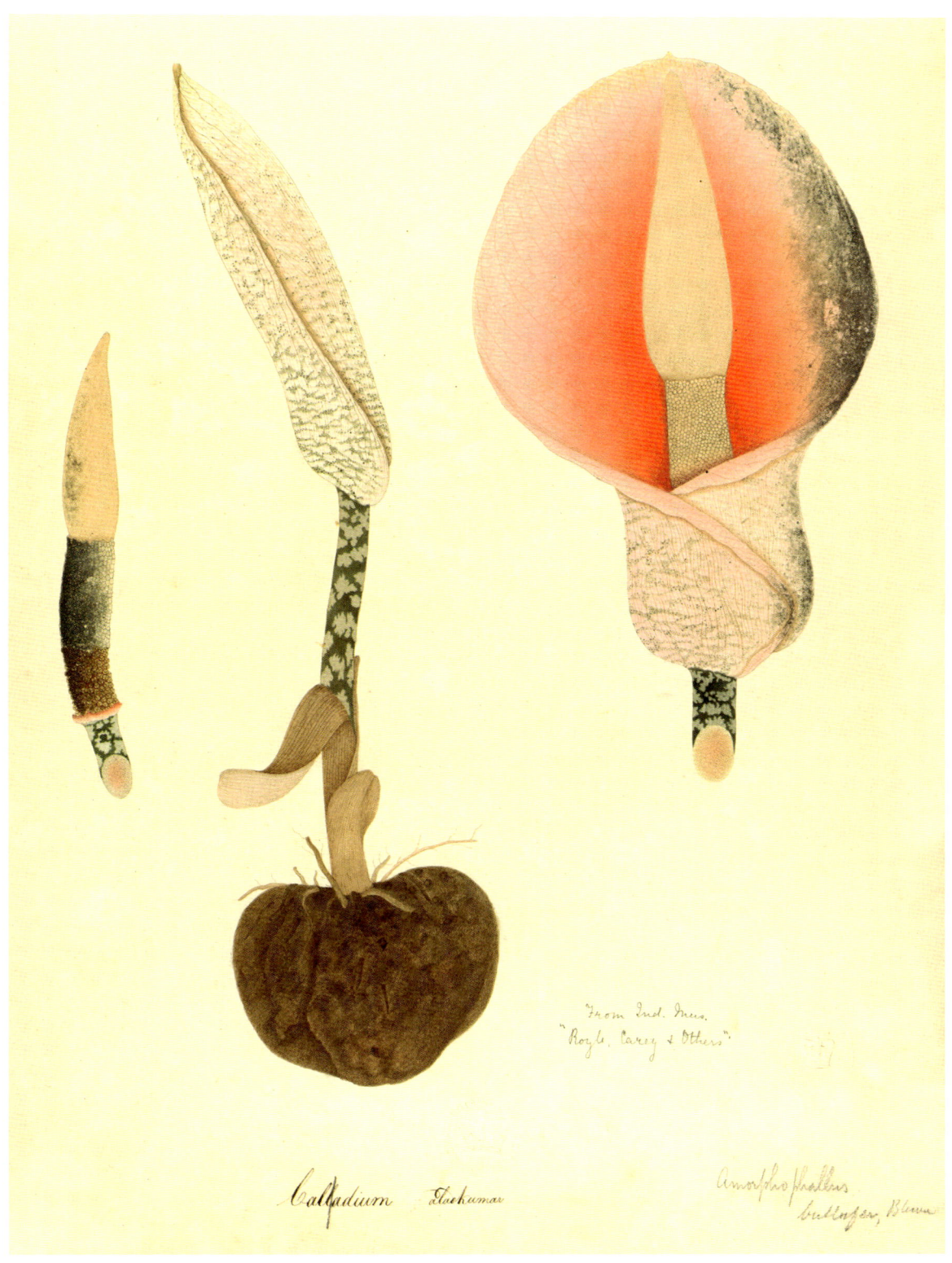

THE CALCUTTA BOTANIC GARDEN, VISHNUPERSAUD, GORACHAND AND NATHANIEL WALLICH

THE CALCUTTA BOTANIC GARDEN WAS THE EARLIEST AND most important of the botanical institutes in India and remained so throughout the 19th century. It was set up in 1786 by Colonel Robert Kyd, a career soldier, but also a keen amateur horticulturist with his own garden around his house 'Shalimar' at Sibpur, near Calcutta. He suggested to the Company that an official garden be set up close to his house, to grow rare plants and to test others for their commercial value, notably spices and medicinal plants that could be used locally or exported to Europe. The site selected was on the west bank of the Hooghly river, and it proved suitable for a wide range of plants, some already grown in India, others imported from as far afield as China and Philadelphia. It was also destined to test out food plants which could alleviate the periodic famines after drought or bad harvests in Madras and Bengal. Very soon the garden became a staging post for exotics brought from China and destined for European gardens. For example, the rose 'Bengal Crimson' was brought to England from Calcutta but, in spite of its name, had originated in a Chinese garden.

ROXBURGH IN CALCUTTA

On the death of Colonel Kyd in 1793, the post of superintendent of the garden at Calcutta was given to William Roxburgh in recognition of the name he had made for himself in Madras. Roxburgh held the job for 20 years, living on the banks of the Hooghly river, in a very grand house that he built in the botanic garden in 1795. While there, he continued with his commissioning of plant portraits, adding to the collection and keeping one copy for himself, with a duplicate sent to the Company in London (this set is now at the Royal Botanic Gardens, Kew).

Roxburgh organised and trained Indian artists to produce botanical paintings in the Calcutta Botanic Garden, as he had in Madras, and there is evidence that his chief Madras artist went with him to Calcutta, but, sadly, his name seems not to have been recorded. In 1804,

Roxburgh's eldest son John, whose mother was Indian, was described as 'head painter', suggesting that he organised a team and taught other artists. John also spent time collecting plants at the Cape of Good Hope and, in 1810, in the Himalayan foothills.

Gardeners were also sent to collect spices, including cloves and nutmeg, from Malacca and other parts of Indonesia, to be cultivated in India, as well as others from the coast of China. Large numbers of seedlings and plants were dispatched around India and to the East Indies, both for forestry, notably teak, and food crops such as the fishtail palm, *Caryota urens*, which could be eaten in times of famine.

Tea was one crop that would be especially valuable if it succeeded in breaking the Chinese monopoly. It had been grown by Colonel Kyd before Roxburgh's arrival, but required a cooler climate than that of Calcutta and Roxburgh's attempts to have it planted in the Himalayan foothills of Bengal came to nothing. More tea plants were collected on Lord Macartney's Embassy to the Emperor Qianlong in 1793 and sent to Calcutta, but these also failed to survive. It was not until 1840 that Chinese tea, introduced to India by Robert Fortune, was successfully cultivated.

Roxburgh finally retired from India in 1813 and reached England in 1814 in a poor state of health. He spent some time in Chelsea, attempting to get his descriptions of Indian plants published, and then went to Edinburgh, where he complained that the cold was 'too hard for an old Indian constitution like mine' and died in February 1815.

Roxburgh's *Icones*, as the plant drawings were called, numbered about 2,542, each with a unique number linked with written descriptions that were published posthumously as *Flora Indica*. In addition to the set of facsimiles of drawings that he sent to the EIC in London, several other

Company employees had copies made, including two Bengal surgeons, John Fleming (now at the Natural History Museum) and James Hare (now at Royal Botanic Garden Edinburgh).

NATHANIEL WALLICH

William Roxburgh's successor in Calcutta was Nathaniel Wallich (1786–1854), who acted as superintendent of the botanic garden from 1817 until 1846. Wallich was Danish, of Jewish parents, and had studied in the Royal Copenhagen Veterinarian School, later qualifying in human medicine. In 1806 he was appointed as a doctor to the Danish settlement at Serampore where he arrived in 1807. With the Napoleonic war raging in Europe, the capture of Copenhagen allowed the Company to take Serampore from the Danes in 1808 and Wallich was taken as a prisoner of war. Roxburgh, who knew him as a good botanist with a wide knowledge of natural history, arranged for him to work in the botanic garden.

As superintendent, Wallich continued Roxburgh's commissioning of botanical paintings, using the same artists, but in his case their names are recorded, notably Gorachand, Ramchand and Vishnupersaud. Wallich published a selection of their drawings, initially in Calcutta, and later on to a much more extensive scale in London.

Wallich himself travelled widely while based in Calcutta: into the Himalaya, visiting Nepal in 1820–21, and the foothills above Dehradun in 1825. In 1822 he visited Penang and Singapore, and Burma in 1826–27, each time accompanied by botanical artists to record the plants collected. Paintings made on their visits to Nepal were published in *Tentamen Florae Napalensis Illustratae. Consisting of botanical illustrations and lithographic figures of select Nipal plants*. This was published in two volumes, in 1824 and 1826, by the Asiatic Lithographic Press in Calcutta.

The botanist John Crawfurd (1783–1868) travelled with Wallich to Burma in 1826, where he is credited with the discovery of the scarlet-flowered leguminous tree, magnificently illustrated for Wallich by Vishnupersaud and named after the governor-general and his wife as *Amherstia nobilis*.

Wallich's great work, *Plantae Asiaticae Rariores or descriptions and figures of a select number of unpublished East Indian plants* was published while he was on leave in London between 1830 and 1832, with 295 lithographs of rare or little-known plants. Only 254 copies of this superb book were printed in grey and hand-coloured using

Gorachand's and Vishnupersaud's original paintings as a guide.

Having survived cholera, Wallich resigned from Calcutta in 1846 due to ill health and went to live in London. There he worked to complete the distribution of the vast herbarium he had assembled in Calcutta, which he had started, along with its lithographed catalogue, during his home leave of 1829–32. He became vice-president of the Linnean Society, as well as a fellow of the Royal Society. The top set of his specimens, the great EIC herbarium with more than 20,000 specimens, is now at the Royal Botanic Gardens, Kew, with duplicates widely dispersed in the world's herbaria. The original plant paintings that he commissioned in Calcutta during the 1820s are also at Kew. Wallich died in London in 1854, aged 68.

WILLIAM GRIFFITH

In his short life Dr William Griffith (1810–1845) made very significant contributions to the study of the Indian flora. He was acting superintendent of the Calcutta Botanic Garden from 1842 until 1844, but is credited with destroying much of the beauty of Wallich's garden with the aim of creating a more scientific layout.

Griffith joined the Company in 1832 as a surgeon in Madras. Three years later he was already well-known as a botanist and was invited to join Wallich and others on an expedition to Assam, to study the wild tea plant that had been found growing in the hills. Griffith also travelled to other parts of India; in the west he reached as far as Bamian in Afghanistan in 1839, and the previous year had been the first major botanist to discover the botanical riches of Bhutan. His extensive notebooks, botanical sketches and diaries were edited after his death by Dr John McClelland, including his *Journals of Travels in Assam, Burma, Bootan, Affghanistan and the Neighbouring Countries* (1847). As well as plants, Griffith studied and collected birds and fish, and had drawings of them made. In many cases, after the specimens had rotted through neglect, the paintings remained as the only record of the original species. Griffith's *Icones Plantarum Asiaticarum*, published in Calcutta in 1847 and 1854, consist of meticulously detailed dissections of plants, lithographed by the Calcutta Botanic Garden artists from his own sketches. His name is commemorated in *Primula griffithii* and *Rhododendron griffithianum* and some of the earliest herbarium specimens from Afghanistan in the herbarium at Kew were collected by him.

The botanical garden in Calcutta is still a valuable green space with wonderful trees, though in truth more of a park than a scientific

garden. It has been renamed the Acharya Jagadish Chandra Bose Indian Botanic Garden, after the physicist and plant scientist A.J.C. Bose (1858–1937), one of the greatest Indian scientists of the early 20th century. Bose was educated at St Xavier's College, Bombay, then studied at London University and at Jesus College, Cambridge, under the physicist Lord Rayleigh, before returning to India to be professor of physics at Calcutta University.

slipper orchid

Paphiopedilum venustum
(as *Cypripedium venustum*)
(Orchidaceae)

Probably by Vishnupersaud, for Nathaniel Wallich in Calcutta before 1820.

When described by John Sims in *Curtis's Botanical Magazine* in 1820, this lovely orchid was said to have been brought from Nepal to the Calcutta Botanic Garden by a Capt. Craigie. It grows on shady banks and moist cliffs at up to 1,600 m, from central Nepal and Bhutan east to Bangladesh and south Tibet.

orchid

Dendrobium densiflorum
(Orchidaceae)

By Vishnupersaud, for Nathaniel Wallich, probably in Nepal, *c.* 1820.

This subtropical epiphytic orchid is popular in cultivation: it is found wild from central Nepal, east to Burma, on trees and rocks in the forest, up to 1,600 m, flowering in the spring. This is the original painting for the plate in Wallich's *Plantae Asiaticae Rariores* t. 40 (1830).

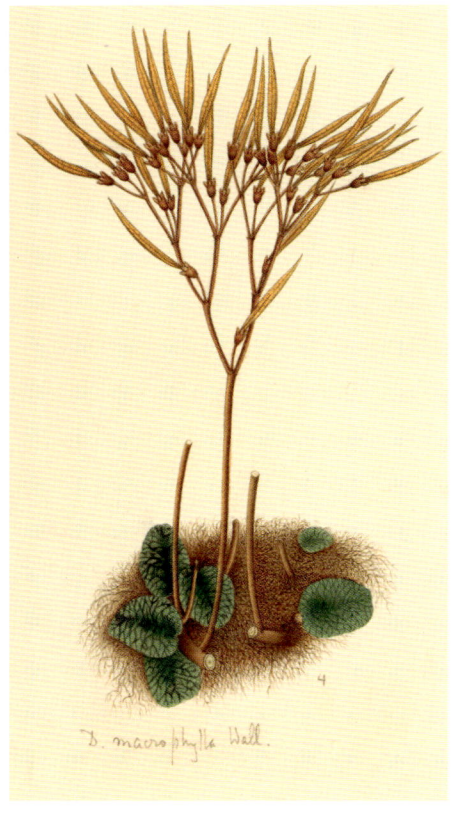

Didymocarpus primulifolius as *D. aromatica* (flowering) and *Didymocarpus macrophyllus* (fruiting) (Gesneriaceae)

By Gorachand, for Nathaniel Wallich in Calcutta, *c.* 1820.

Both these species grow on shady, wet rocks in the forest, flowering in the summer. This is the original painting for the plate in Wallich's *Plantae Asiaticae Rariores* t. 141 (1831).

Detail of the fruit from the adjacent painting.

pajanelia or pajneli →

Pajanelia longifolia (as *Bignonia multijuga*) (Bignoniaceae)

By Vishnupersaud, for Nathaniel Wallich in Calcutta, *c.* 1820.

This large tree, to 30 m tall, is common in mountain forests in eastern India, extending to Thailand, Sumatra and Borneo. Wallich found it near Sylhet, and it was brought into Calcutta Botanic Garden in 1818. The leaves are 60–90 cm long, and the inflorescence to 120 cm tall; its flowers are very stiff, probably to survive visits by bats which are its likely pollinators. This is the original painting for the plate in Wallich's *Plantae Asiaticae Rariores* t. 95 & 96 (1830).

evergreen magnolia

Magnolia pterocarpa (as *Liriodendron grandiflora*) (Magnoliaceae)

Artist unknown, for Nathaniel Wallich in Calcutta, *c.* 1820.

William Roxburgh found this magnolia in the forests of Silhet and Chittagong, (and it is known also from the terai forests of Nepal and Sikkim) 'where it blossoms in April and May, and perfumes the air to a considerable distance with the fragrance of its fine large flowers.' *Plants of the Coast of Coromandel* 3(3): 62, t. 266 (1819). The large, cone-like fruits have long projecting scales which recurve as the seeds ripen.

evergreen oak

Lithocarpus elegans (as *Quercus spicata*) (Leguminosae)

By Vishnupersaud, for Nathaniel Wallich in Calcutta, c. 1820.

A common oak in the warm forests below 2,200 m, from Nepal to Sikkim and northern Assam, extending east to Malesia. The tree can reach 20 m or more; the acorns are edible, thickly packed on spikes about 20 cm long. This is the original painting for the plate in Wallich's *Plantae Asiaticae Rariores* t. 46 (1830).

Burmese lacquer

Gluta usitata (previously called *Melanorrhoea usitata*) (Anacardiaceae)

By Vishnupersaud, for Nathaniel Wallich in Calcutta, *c.* 1827.

The resin of this large deciduous tree is an important source of a black, hard varnish, used to make lacquer ware (Yun-de) in Burma. Wild trees are found in the teak forests from Manipur and Burma to Thailand and Vietnam, and are spectacular early in the year when the leafless trees have bright red flowers followed by fruit with persistent, enlarged petals. This is the original painting for the plates in Wallich's *Plantae Asiaticae Rariores* t. 11 & 12 (1830).

pink ball tree

Dombeya wallichii (Malvaceae)

Artist unknown, for Nathaniel Wallich in Calcutta, *c.* 1820.

In 1821 John Lindley named this species after Wallich, who sent specimens to London from Calcutta. It was then considered a most exciting exotic for heated greenhouses. Nowadays it is widely cultivated in frost-free climates. It appears to have originated in Madagascar, but may also be native or long-cultivated in India. The hanging heads of flowers are around 10 cm across.

anyaar
Lyonia ovalifolia (Ericaceae)

By Vishnupersaud, for Nathaniel Wallich in Nepal in 1820.

This shrub is common in oak and rhododendron forests from northern Pakistan to southern China, at up to 3,000 m, flowering in April and May. The leaves are poisonous and avoided by animals, and are used as an insecticide in cattle stalls. This is the original painting for the plate in Wallich's description of *Andromeda ovalifolia*, in *Asiatic Researches* 13: 390 (1820).

← dogwood
Cornus capitata (Cornaceae)

By Gorachand, for Nathaniel Wallich in Calcutta, *c.* 1820.

Wallich first found this tree on Mount Chandaghiry (Kandrang Garhi) near Kathmandu in Nepal, but it is now known along the Himalaya from Himachal Pradesh to Sichuan in south-west China, growing at altitudes up to 3,400 m. The minute flowers are in a tight head, with 4 or 5 petal-like bracts. The fruits are fleshy with a few hard seeds and, though rather tasteless, are used for making preserves.

This is the original painting for the plate in Wallich's *Plantae Asiaticae Rariores* t. 214 (1832).

three-petal balsam

Impatiens tripetala
(Balsaminaceae)

Artist unknown, for Nathaniel Wallich in Calcutta, *c.* 1820.

Balsam, the genus *Impatiens*, is one of the largest in the Indian flora with 210 species, mostly in the foothills of the Himalaya and in the Western Ghats. Many botanists were fascinated by the diversity of species, notably Joseph Hooker, who after visiting India as a young naturalist spent the rest of his life studying all the species. His signature can be seen after the names on both these paintings. In recent years, especially in England, one eastern Himalayan species, *I. glandulifera*, has a bad name as a tall and invasive weed growing along rivers.

→

balsam

Impatiens bracteata
(Balsaminaceae)

Artist unknown, for Nathaniel Wallich in Calcutta, *c.* 1820.

This balsam is remarkable for its very finely divided bracts, which appear almost woolly. It is native of the Khasi Hills in Assam, but has become naturalised in other areas, notably in Darjeeling.

JOHN FORBES ROYLE AND VISHNUPERSAUD AT SAHARANPUR

THE BOTANIST JOHN FORBES ROYLE (1798–1858) IS USUALLY associated with the flora of the Himalayan mountains from Kumaon as far west as Kashmir. Like so many others, Royle was Scottish by ancestry, though he was actually born in Cawnpore (Kanpur); he was sent to school in Edinburgh and trained at the EIC Military Academy at Addiscombe (much later obtaining an MD from Munich in 1833). He joined the Company as a surgeon in Bengal in 1819 and in 1823 was appointed superintendent of the Company's garden at Saharanpur, in the north-west, near Dehradun in the foothills of the Himalaya. This had been started as a pleasure garden by the Rohilla chieftain Zabita Khan, but was established as a botanic garden in 1819, concentrating on medicinal plants, especially those from the mountains. From the 1840s it became one of the most important locations for the introduction of tea to India.

Royle travelled widely in the western Himalaya and in 1828, while Wallich was on leave, he employed the Calcutta Botanic Garden artists, including Vishnupersaud and Luchman Singh, to make paintings. Royle returned to England in 1831, and later became professor of materia medica at King's College, London. A hundred of the plant paintings he commissioned, most by Vishnupersaud, were published in *Illustrations of the Botany and Other Branches of the Natural History of the Himalayan Mountains*, published between 1833 and 1840. The plates were lithographed in London by Maxim Gauci, then hand-coloured, and the book is valuable as the first study of the ecology of the area, and of the distribution of plant families and genera in the Himalaya. Most of the original paintings are at the Royal Botanic Gardens, Kew.

CHRISTIAN, COUNTESS OF DALHOUSIE AT SIMLA

While staying in Simla in 1827, Christian Ramsay, Countess of Dalhousie, née Broun (1786–1839) commissioned an Indian artist to make 75 plant drawings, now at Kew. A keen botanist, she was in India as wife of the commander-in-chief of the EIC army. Her son became the Marquess of Dalhousie, a somewhat controversial governor-general, in whose company Joseph Hooker travelled to India in 1848. The drawings depict temperate plants of the central and western Himalaya including *Lilium polyphyllum*, and are interesting in bearing Hindi inscriptions giving the plant's local name and flowering time.

In Simla, Lady Dalhousie was friendly with Dr George Govan and his wife Mary (née Maitland). Govan was the first superintendent of the Saharanpur Garden (from 1819 to 1823). After a home leave to Scotland, he returned to India with his newly acquired wife and in the 1820s, while based in Simla, the Govans assembled a large collection of drawings, mostly by Indian artists, but some by Mary herself. Some of Lady Dalhousie's drawings were copied from the Govan collection.

During her Indian sojourn of 1829–32, Lady Dalhousie also made plant collections around Simla, and in other parts of the Himalaya; her Indian herbarium specimens are now at Edinburgh.

black pea

Thermopsis barbata
(Leguminosae)

By Vishnupersaud, for John Royle, Saharanpur, *c.* 1828.

A lupin-like mountain plant with unusual purple-black flowers, found above 3,000 m. This is the original painting for the plate in Royle's *Illustrations of the Botany and Other Branches of the Natural History of the Himalayan Mountains, and of the Flora of Cashmere* vol. 1: t. 47 (1839).

←
knotweeds

Bistorta vacciniifolia and *B. affinis* (as *Polygonum brunonis*)
(Polygonaceae)

Artist unknown, for John Royle, Saharanpur, *c.* 1828.

Both these are high mountain plants, usually growing above 3,000 m.

spikenard
Nardostachys jatamansi (Caprifoliaceae)

Artist unknown, for John Royle, Saharanpur, *c.* 1828.

The aromatic oil of spikenard is extracted from the roots of this plant. It is valued for its medicinal use as a sedative, a hair tonic and as incense in religious ceremonies. Because it is so valuable, this plant is endangered, even though it grows high in the Himalayas, above 3,600 m. This is the original painting for the plate in Royle's *Illustrations of the Botany and Other Branches of the Natural History of the Himalayan Mountains, and of the Flora of Cashmere* vol. 2: t. 52 (1839).

→

mountain rhubarb
Rheum spiciforme (Polygonaceae)

By Vishnupersaud, for John Royle, Saharanpur, *c.* 1828.

A widespread perennial herb, growing on rather dry slopes in the Himalaya above 3,600 m, from Afghanistan to Bhutan and Tibet. This is the original painting for the plate in Royle's *Illustrations of the Botany and Other Branches of the Natural History of the Himalayan Mountains, and of the Flora of Cashmere* vol. 2: t. 78 (1839).

wild ginger
Hedychium coccineum (Zingiberaceae)

A Calcutta artist, for John Royle, Saharanpur, *c.* 1828.

A decorative plant from wet, subtropical and temperate forests in the foothills of Bhutan, Darjeeling and Sikkim, at up to 2,000 m, drawn from a plant growing in Mussoorie.

Agapetes variegata (as *Thiebaudia variegata*) (Ericaceae)

Artist unknown, probably for Nathaniel Wallich, in Calcutta.

An epiphytic shrub flowering in November in the warm-temperate forests of the Himalaya, from Bhutan eastwards to Thailand. The name *variegata* refers to the flowers, which often have transverse zigzag lines across the corolla. This is the original painting for the plate in Royle's *Illustrations of the Botany and Other Branches of the Natural History of the Himalayan Mountains, and of the Flora of Cashmere* vol. 2: t. 63a (1839).

Strobilanthes attenuata (Acanthaceae)

Artist unknown, for Lady Christian Dalhousie in Simla, *c.* 1830.

An autumn-flowering perennial, found wild in foothills of the western Himalaya from Afghanistan to Uttaranchal, and common in the forests around Simla. A related species *S. cusia* kuntze is used as an indigo dye in Assam and eastwards into Yunnan.

←

chir pine

Pinus roxburghii (as *P. longifolia*) (Pinaceae)

A Calcutta artist, for John Royle, Saharanpur, *c.* 1828.

Chir pine is found in dry valleys at up to 2,000 m, from Afghanistan along the Himalaya to Burma. Trees can reach 30 m and the needles which are in threes can be 30 cm long, hanging down from the twigs. This is the original painting for the plate in Royle's *Illustrations of the Botany and Other Branches of the Natural History of the Himalayan Mountains, and of the Flora of Cashmere* vol. 2: t. 85 (1839).

JOHN FORBES ROYLE & VISHNUPERSAUD 151

peach tree
Prunus persica (Rosaceae)

Artist unknown, or perhaps by Mrs Govan in Simla, *c.* 1830.

The peach and the nectarine (a variety of peach with smooth-skinned fruit) originate in northern China. They grow well in India in areas where the winters are cold enough for the trees to become deciduous, that is mainly in the hills, both in the north-west and the north-east.

wild larkspur or jadwar
probably *Delphinium denudatum* (Ranunculaceae)

Artist unknown, for Lady Christian Dalhousie in Simla, *c.* 1830.

This is a common plant in the hills of northern India, and the dried roots are widely used medicinally.

Himalayan bird cherry

Prunus cornuta (Rosaceae)

Artist unknown, or perhaps by Mrs Govan in Simla, *c*. 1830.

The Latin name for this tree refers to the horn-like galls produced by infection with the fungus *Taphrina padi*, shown in this painting with the normal flowers and fruit. The Himalayan bird cherry makes an upright deciduous tree to around 15 m high, and is widespread in the mountains above around 2,500 m, from Afghanistan to Sikkim and southern Tibet.

shoo-fly plant

Nicandra physalodes (Solanaceae)

Artist unknown, or perhaps by Mrs Govan in Simla, *c*. 1830.

A native of South America, but now a common weed in warm areas around the world. The whole plant is poisonous, but has been used as an insecticide and, in small doses, as a medicine.

fennel, hing or asafoetida →

Ferula narthex (Apiaceae)

Artist unknown, or perhaps by Mrs Govan in Simla, *c*. 1830.

This is a large perennial that grows wild in dry areas of the western Himalaya, notably in Kashmir and Ladakh. The young leaves are widely used as a medicine to aid digestion and reduce flatulence. It is one of several species from which the spice asafoetida is obtained.

It was first grown in Edinburgh in 1839 from seeds sent by Dr Hugh Falconer from Ladakh.

HUGH FALCONER AND THE CALCUTTA BOTANICAL ARTISTS IN SAHARANPUR

HUGH FALCONER (1808–1865) WAS SUPERINTENDENT OF THE Botanic Garden at Saharanpur from 1832, and then from 1841 in Calcutta, where he restored much of the beauty of the gardens following Griffith's clearances; he also held the post of professor of botany in the Calcutta Medical College from 1848 until 1855. Falconer was another medical graduate from Edinburgh, who joined the EIC as an assistant surgeon in 1830. He is best remembered as a palaeontologist and friend of Charles Darwin, but was also an important advisor to the Company on economic plants, helping to establish the cultivation of tea, the planting of *Cinchona* for the production of quinine, and campaigning to prevent the wholesale felling of the teak forests of Tennaserim in the south of Burma.

A large collection of plant drawings at the Royal Botanic Gardens, Kew were commissioned by Falconer. About half of them were made by the Calcutta Botanic Garden artists, who were still at Saharanpur when Falconer took over from Royle in 1832. The collection includes a large number of orchids from the Himalayan foothills, as well as many grasses and sedges. Some of the paintings are signed by Vishnupersaud and Luchman Singh, others by Cassim Ali. Falconer was superintendent in Calcutta during Joseph Hooker's Indian visit in 1850, and Hooker commemorated his friend's name in the spectacular, large-leaved *Rhododendron falconeri*. The grass specialist William Munro named the bamboo now known as *Himalayacalamus falconeri* for him.

Page 157

bamboo
Himalayacalamus falconeri
(Poaceae)

Artist unknown, for Hugh Falconer, in the Botanic Garden at Saharanpur, c. 1835.

This bamboo is shown in flower: most bamboos flower very rarely, once in 20 to 100 years, and all plants of one species tend to flower the same year. However, we know that this species was also flowering in 1821, as there is a specimen from that date in the herbarium in Edinburgh, collected by Nathaniel Wallich. Like many bamboos, the young shoots are edible.

mahonia
Mahonia napaulensis
(Berberidaceae)

Artist unknown, for Hugh Falconer in the Botanic Garden at Saharanpur, c. 1832.

This winter-flowering shrub is found from western Nepal to West Bengal and Bhutan growing in mountain forests. The sweetly-scented flowers are followed by blue berries.

shieldfern
Polystichum squarrosum (Dryopteridaceae)

By Vishnupersaud, for Hugh Falconer, in the Botanic Garden at Saharanpur, c. 1835.

This beautiful drawing was first identified as *Polystichum aculeatum*, a temperate species from Europe and Asia.

cassia indigo or kathi
Indigofera cassioides (Leguminosae)

Artist unknown, for Hugh Falconer, in the Botanic Garden at Saharanpur, c. 1835.

There are several, very similar shrubby *Indigofera* species, usually found in rather dry valleys in the Himalayas. This species is an attractive shrub, found on dry hills from Pakistan and India (including the south), east to Yunnan and Guangxi. The leaves and flowers can be eaten: the roots used medicinally.

orchid

Cyrtosia falconeri (Orchidaceae)

Artist unknown, for Hugh Falconer, in the Botanic Garden at Saharanpur, *c.* 1835.

This spectacular orchid has no leaves or green shoots and is entirely saprophytic. Its stems can reach 3 m high, with flowers around 3.5 cm across. Falconer collected it in mountain woods in Garwhal and at present it is known from the Himalayas, Thailand and southern China.

orchid →

Phalaenopsis taenialis (Orchidaceae)

Artist unknown, for Hugh Falconer, in the Botanic Garden at Saharanpur, *c.* 1835.

This orchid does most of its photosynthesis in its roots which are extensive and flattened so as to be about 8 mm wide, spreading over the surface of tree trunks; the leaves and flowers are quite small, about 2 cm across. It has been recorded from Kumaon east to Burma and Yunnan.

winter bergenia

Bergenia ciliata f. *ligulata* (Saxifragaceae)

Artist unknown, for Hugh Falconer, in the Botanic Garden at Saharanpur, *c.* 1835.

This large perennial is common on rocky mountain slopes and in forests from Afghanistan to southeast Tibet, reaching 4,300 m in Kashmir. It forms spreading mats across the ground, flowering in early spring or as soon as the snow has melted. This is also called *Bergenia pacumbis,* the name taken from the Nepali name for the plant, pakhanbet. The plant can be used medicinally.

orchid

Calanthe tricarinata (Orchidaceae)

Artist unknown, for Hugh Falconer, in the Botanic Garden at Saharanpur, *c.* 1835.

Orchids of the genus *Calanthe* are widely grown as ornamentals. This is a widespread species found in mossy forests from Pakistan to south-west China and Japan.

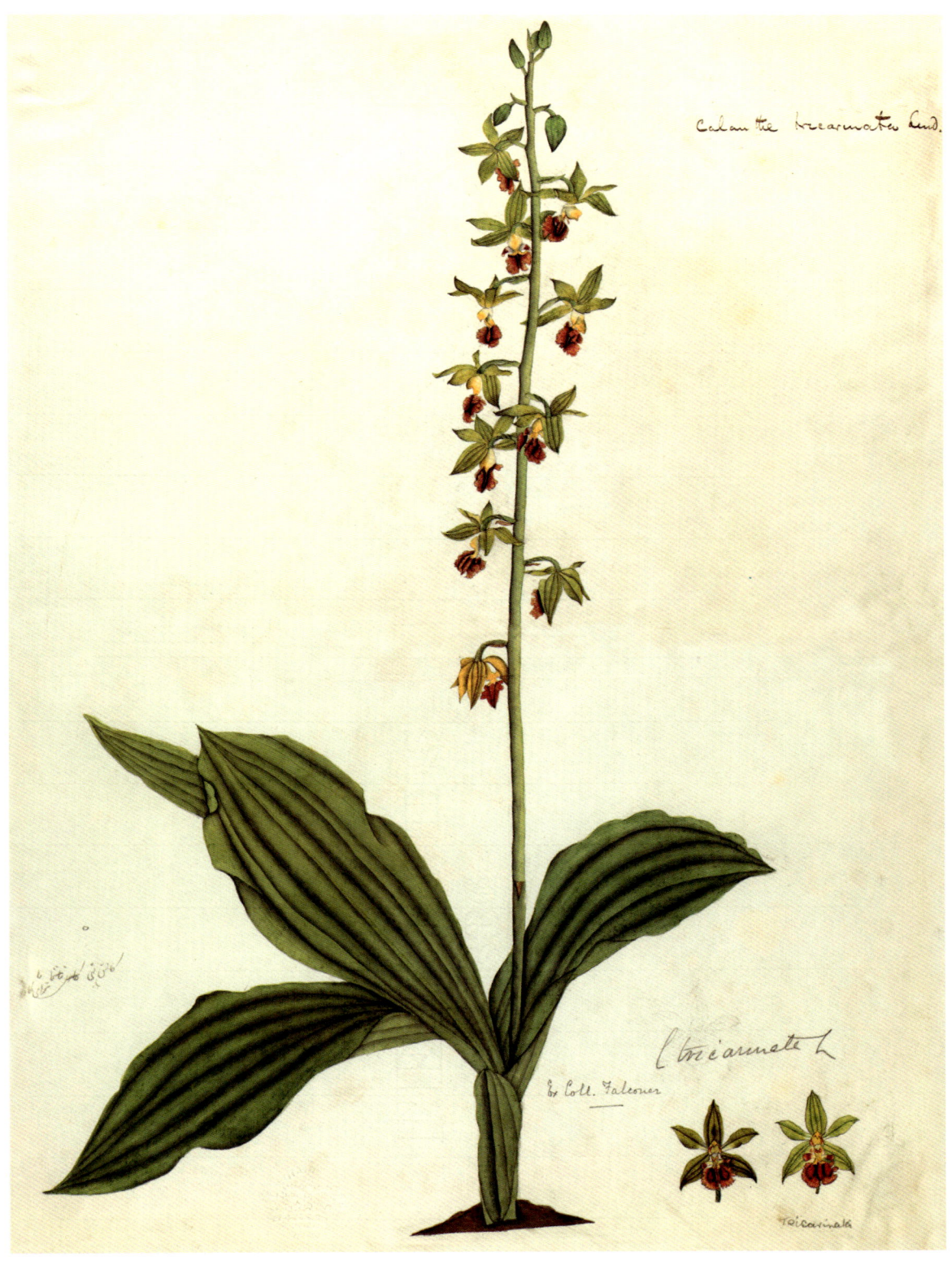

JOHN FERGUSON CATHCART AND JOSEPH HOOKER IN DARJEELING

ONE OF THE MOST BEAUTIFUL BOTANICAL BOOKS EVER produced was that orchestrated by Joseph Hooker, using paintings commissioned by John Ferguson Cathcart (1802–51). Cathcart, son of a Scottish judge, was a member of the Bengal Civil Service who arrived in Calcutta in 1822, but his health gave out, and thereafter he lived in Darjeeling where he created a botanical garden around his house. This occupied a spur overlooking the gorge of the Rangeet river, with paths cut through the forest, and collections of climbers, orchids, aroids and ferns. Here he employed a team of Indian artists to record the plants brought to him from the mountains by local Lepcha collectors.

Joseph Hooker visited him in 1848 and was impressed by the collection of paintings, as he wrote to his father: 'Cathcart's drawings, I have surely explained, are all now going on with being made at or near Darjeeling, of Darjeeling plants. He has five artists at work, who turn out together about three plants a week – it costs him more than all my pay together'. As Cathcart explained to Hooker, he 'intended to procure more artists, the best that could be obtained, from Calcutta, especially those skilled ones, who had been trained under Wallich and Griffith in the Botanic Garden, and to draw every plant of interest that he or I could procure'.

The drawings eventually numbered over a thousand, though they were clearly produced in great haste and the majority are only partly coloured, doubtless with the intention of later completion. Hooker promised to have some of the drawings published but, in the meanwhile, in 1851, Cathcart had died in Lausanne, Switzerland, on his way home to Scotland. Hooker was given the original drawings by Cathcart's sister and he arranged to have a small selection lithographed by Walter Hood Fitch, then chief artist at the Royal Botanic Gardens, Kew. Fitch redrew them onto the stone and 'corrected the stiffness', as well as adding botanical details from

Hooker's dried specimens. Fitch was brilliant at drawing a plant with speed, and in a naturalistic style, producing three-dimensional drawings from flattened herbarium specimens. Just as he had with Hooker's own *Rhododendron* sketches, Fitch adapted Cathcart's drawings, though many might prefer the subtlety of Cathcart's artists' studies (shown here) to Fitch's spectacular rendering of the *Magnolia campbellii* flowers in the printed version.

The beautiful opening page of Cathcart's book has a wreath of Himalayan flowers, bamboos and palms surrounding the title *Illustrations of Himalayan Plants, chiefly selected from drawings made for the late J. F. Cathcart, Esq., of the Bengal Civil Service. The description and analyses by J. D. Hooker M.D. F.R.S. the plates executed by W. H. Fitch.* Published in London in 1855 it contains 24 hand-coloured lithographs of a range of the visually most attractive plants, though these represent only a very small proportion of the whole collection. They include flowering trees, such as *Magnolia campbellii*, shrubs such as *Buddleja colvilei* and herbs, such as the bizarre, cream-bracted spires of *Rheum nobile*. The book's 176 subscribers included Queen Victoria, the Raja of Burdwan, Charles Darwin and the French botanist Alphonse de Candolle. Hooker's introduction provides a eulogy and brief biography of Cathcart, who was born in Edinburgh and attended the University of Leiden. Another large collection of drawings commissioned by Cathcart has recently been identified at the Royal Botanic Garden Edinburgh, smaller in scale but much more finished paintings than those at the Royal Botanic Gardens, Kew.

JOSEPH DALTON HOOKER AND THE RHODODENDRONS OF SIKKIM-HIMALAYA

Through his energy and influence in botanical circles both in Britain and its then thriving Empire, Joseph Dalton Hooker (1817-1911) did as

Frontispiece for the book *Illustrations of Himalayan Plants*.

much as anyone to further the cause of Indian botany in the second half of the 19th century. Hooker was 30 when he visited India for himself, already hardened by four years spent circumnavigating the Antarctic as surgeon-naturalist on HMS *Erebus*, as part of an expedition undertaking research on the magnetic South Pole. He landed in Calcutta in January 1848, on the same ship as the incoming governor-general, Lord Dalhousie (son of the botanist discussed earlier), a contact that was later to prove useful. Hugh Falconer, superintendent of the Calcutta Botanic Garden, recommended that his younger colleague explore Sikkim, then an independent kingdom. In April he went to Darjeeling, then becoming popular as a hill station for Europeans to escape the worst of the summer heat in the plains. Here he met two Scots with natural historical interests – Dr Archibald Campbell, superintendent of the sanatorium and John Cathcart, mentioned above.

Hooker's first journey to the mountains lasted from October 1848 until January 1849, during which he visited the eastern parts of Nepal, reaching to the snow line, and finding signs that the climate was becoming warmer. From Nepal he entered Sikkim, where he met up with Campbell and together they managed to obtain an interview with the Raja of Sikkim. Later that year, in May, they started for the high parts of Sikkim, though following a delay by the dewan who was suspicious of their intentions and wished to keep all trade with Tibet under his own control. Although beset by incessant rain, leeches, and stinging flies, Hooker found the flora rich beyond his dreams, and took particular interest in the gradual changes in the vegetation as the environment changed from subtropical to temperate. Above 3,000 metres the plants were entirely temperate.

In early October Hooker returned to central Sikkim, where he again met Campbell, and the pair travelled to the Tibetan border and in spite of the dewan's order not to cross into Tibet, negotiated with the border guards to remain in that country for a day, before returning to Gangtok. This violation of the border was used by the dewan as a pretext to imprison both, and they were only released after the British government threatened to invade Sikkim. The following year Hooker went into the Khasi Hills with Dr Thomas Thomson, a college friend from Glasgow days, where they found the unique blue orchid, *Vanda coerulea*. They reached the border of Manipur, and then returned to Calcutta, from where Hooker travelled to England in early 1851.

Hooker was amazed by the quantity and number of rhododendron species in Sikkim and made sketches of many of them in the field. Some of these sketches were dispatched from Darjeeling to his father at the Royal Botanic Gardens, Kew, who asked the Kew botanical artist Walter Hood Fitch to develop them into finished lithographs. The result was *The Rhododendrons of the Sikkim-Himalaya*, the first part of which was published in 1849 while Hooker was still in Sikkim; the second part came out in 1851. In total there are 30 large plates of new species. This book, together with Hooker's *Himalayan Journals*, an account of his journeys, changed the face of gardens in England, Scotland and Ireland – with plantations of rhododendrons, magnolias, bamboos, pines and deodars, they came to resemble Indian hill stations. As well as bringing back herbarium specimens of dried plants, Hooker sent home thousands of seeds, and started his own collection of botanical paintings, which he augmented whenever possible after he was back at Kew. These were to culminate in *The Flora of British India*, a collaboration with others, published from 1875 onwards.

As director of the Royal Botanic Gardens, Kew in succession to his father, Joseph Hooker had a wide range of botanical contacts around the world, but particularly in India, and he built up the herbarium at Kew to international size and status. It was for this reason that when the museum and library collections made by the Company were being dispersed in 1879, much of the material, both botanical paintings and specimens, were sent to Kew, where they are still available for study.

The great Temperate House at Kew, which opened in 1863, was designed to grow plants that needed little heat, but shelter from wind and hard frost. The conditions in much of the house aim to mimic the cool moist climate found in the foothills of the Himalaya or tropical hill stations, to grow the more delicate species of *Rhododendron*, tree ferns and bamboos that became so fashionable in the late 19th century.

Hooker's friendship with Lord Dalhousie and his wife Susan stood him in good stead while travelling around India. By way of thanks Hooker named one of his most beautiful new rhododendrons, with large, scented white flowers, *Rhododendron dalhousieae* in Susan's honour. Sadly, she became ill soon after arriving in Bengal, a stay in the hills of Ceylon failed to restore her health, and she died on board ship on the way home to Scotland in 1853.

tree magnolia
Magnolia campbellii (Magnoliaceae)

Artist unknown, for John Cathcart in Darjeeling, *c.* 1850.

This is one of the most spectacular of all temperate trees, covered with flowers in early spring on bare branches before the leaves open. In Nepal the flowers are usually white, whereas this pink form, with flowers 20 cm or more across, is commoner in Sikkim and the eastern Himalayas. At the time of Hooker's visit, the trees were very common around Darjeeling, colouring the hills with pink and crimson flowers.

Didymocarpus aurantiacus (Gesneriaceae)

Artist unknown, for John Cathcart in Darjeeling, *c.* 1850.

Many beautiful species in the family Gesneriaceae are found in warm, moist forests in the hills of India, but are seldom cultivated. This rarity was found 'by the way-side in the well-known road from Darjeeling to the Runjeet cane bridge'. It is mainly the East African gesneriads such as the African violets (*Saintpaulia*) and hybrids of *Streptocarpus* that are so popular as houseplants.

←
orchid
Cymbidium elegans (Orchidaceae)

Artist unknown, for John Cathcart in Darjeeling, *c.* 1850.

This spectacular orchid with crowded hanging spikes of flowers to 60 cm long is found on trees and rocks in damp forests in the mountains, from Nepal to Yunnan and Sichuan.

balsam
Impatiens spirifera (Balsaminaceae)

Artist unknown, for John Cathcart in Darjeeling, *c.* 1850.

India has more different and varied species of *Impatiens* than any other country, and this one has a creeping stem rooting as it trails along the ground and relatively large flowers. The name refers to the spiral spur.

crimson cherry

Prunus carmesina (Rosaceae)

Artist unknown, for John Cathcart in Darjeeling, *c.* 1850.

This beautiful cherry flowers in early spring on leafless branches. It is widespread in the Himalayas from western Nepal to Bhutan, Sikkim and Yunnan, and can make a large tree to 30 m; the dark purple, cherry-like fruits are edible.

Aeschynanthus peelii (Gesneriaceae)

Artist unknown, for John Cathcart in Darjeeling, *c.* 1850.

These striking plants have fleshy leaves and creeping stems rooting and hanging down from trees or rocks in the forest, in Bhutan and near Darjeeling. The red, tubular flowers suggest that it is pollinated by birds. This painting was used in Cathcart's *Illustrations of Himalayan Plants*. *Aeschynanthus peelii* is sometimes considered a mere variety of *A. bracteatus*.

Actinidia strigosa
(Actinidiaceae)

Artist unknown, for John Cathcart in Darjeeling, *c.* 1850.

This climber is a relative of the Chinese *A. chinensis*, widely cultivated as Chinese gooseberry or kiwi fruit in New Zealand. In *A. strigosa*, found in Bhutan and Sikkim, the whole plant is bristly-hairy, and the cylindrical fruits are edible, about 6 cm long, purplish when ripe. *A. callosa* is very similar, but less hairy.

→
clematis
Clematis grewiiflora
(Ranunculaceae)

Artist unknown, for John Cathcart in Darjeeling, *c.* 1850.

This clematis is a strong-growing woody climber, found in warm dry forest in Bhutan, Sikkim and around Darjeeling. The whole plant is covered with brown hairs. The artist here has enjoyed filling the page with the trailing stems and flowers, a style typical of many of the Indian botanical artists.

shrubby milkwort
Polygala arillata (Polygalaceae)

Artist unknown, for John Cathcart in Darjeeling, *c.* 1850.

Though European milkworts are all small annuals or perennials, there are several woody species in the Himalaya and in South Africa. *P. arillata* is one of the most common and is very widespread, forming a shrub or small tree growing in scrub and along forest paths, from Nepal to south-west China, and in south India, Sri Lanka and the Philippines.

→
rhododendron
Rhododendron edgeworthii (Ericaceae)

Hand-coloured lithograph by W.H. Fitch after a field sketch by Joseph Hooker, from Hooker's *Rhododendrons of the Sikkim Himalaya* (1849–51).

This beautiful rhododendron grows on trees such as evergreen oaks and on rocks by streams from Sikkim and Bhutan to Yunnan. The flowers are deliciously scented. Hooker named this species after Michael Pakenham Edgeworth (1812–81), an Irish botanist, pioneer photographer and authority on the flora of north-west India, who was at that time commissioner of Multan in the Punjab. Edgeworth studied both botany and Indian languages at Edinburgh, before joining the East India Company in 1831.

rhododendron

Rhododendron thomsonii (Ericaceae)

Hand-coloured lithograph by W.H. Fitch after a field sketch by Joseph Hooker, from Hooker's *Rhododendrons of the Sikkim Himalaya* (1849–51).

This rhododendron is recognised by its smooth and flaking bark, almost round bluish-green leaves, and waxy, red flowers. It is found in eastern Nepal, Sikkim and Bhutan as well as in the area of Darjeeling, and is common in many areas in conifer woods and above the forest line to 4,000 m. Hooker named it after his childhood friend in Glasgow, Dr Thomas Thomson (1817–78) who travelled with him in the Himalaya, and after a career as an army surgeon, became superintendent of the Calcutta Botanic Garden.

→

high alpine rhododendrons

Rhododendron salignum and *R. eleagnoides* (Ericaceae)

Hand-coloured lithograph by W.H. Fitch after a field sketch by Joseph Hooker, from Hooker's *Rhododendrons of the Sikkim Himalaya* (1849–51).

Rhododendrons grow at all altitudes in the Himalaya, forming large trees or epiphytes in the warmer forests, to dwarf, gnarled shrubs in bare places above the tree line. Hooker named these two species after shrubs with similar leaves, *R. salignum* after the willow, and *R. eleagnoides* after *Eleagnus*. Both species are now considered to belong to *R. lepidotum*, which can have flowers in any shade of white, yellow, pink, red or purple, and extends from Kashmir to Yunnan, usually at over 2,500 m.

ROBERT WIGHT, RUNGIAH AND GOVINDOO IN MADRAS

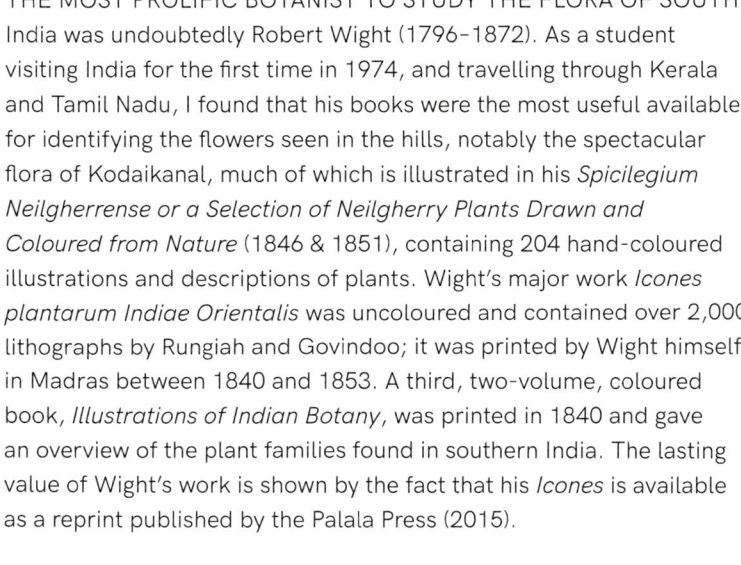

THE MOST PROLIFIC BOTANIST TO STUDY THE FLORA OF SOUTH India was undoubtedly Robert Wight (1796–1872). As a student visiting India for the first time in 1974, and travelling through Kerala and Tamil Nadu, I found that his books were the most useful available for identifying the flowers seen in the hills, notably the spectacular flora of Kodaikanal, much of which is illustrated in his *Spicilegium Neilgherrense or a Selection of Neilgherry Plants Drawn and Coloured from Nature* (1846 & 1851), containing 204 hand-coloured illustrations and descriptions of plants. Wight's major work *Icones plantarum Indiae Orientalis* was uncoloured and contained over 2,000 lithographs by Rungiah and Govindoo; it was printed by Wight himself in Madras between 1840 and 1853. A third, two-volume, coloured book, *Illustrations of Indian Botany*, was printed in 1840 and gave an overview of the plant families found in southern India. The lasting value of Wight's work is shown by the fact that his *Icones* is available as a reprint published by the Palala Press (2015).

Wight arrived in India in 1819 after graduating in medicine from Edinburgh University the previous year. After landing in Madras he was appointed garrison surgeon to the 21st regiment of Madras Native Infantry at Masulipatnam, famous since classical times for the production of muslin. He remained here until 1824, when he was made veterinary surgeon for Tipu Sultan's cattle-breeding station in Mysore, a huge establishment containing about 30,000 cattle and providing bullocks for heavy transport. After a year there Wight became sick, and resigned this post, and was then appointed assistant surgeon to another regiment, stationed in Vellore. All this time Wight was studying the local plants and building up a herbarium, and this resulted in his being appointed Madras naturalist and botanist in 1826. This position had been filled by Patrick Russell in the late 1780s, and then by William Roxburgh before he moved to Calcutta.

As soon as his appointment was confirmed, Wight planned a long tour of his area, with portable plant presses, tin-lined boxes and an artist

to record the plants in detail and colour. This took him into the hills and as far as the Kerala coast at Trivandrum (Thiruvananthapuram) and Alleppey (Alappuzha). The results were considerable, consisting of thousands of plant specimens as well as insects, birds and geological samples, and Wight planned an even longer trip for the following year, so it was a particular tragedy that the new governor of Madras summarily abolished the naturalist's post in January 1828. Wight went back to being an army surgeon, but his collections were dispatched to the Company in London and have survived, mostly at the Royal Botanic Gardens, Kew and the Royal Botanic Garden Edinburgh. His next position was in Negapatam (Nagapattinam), near Tanjore (Thanjavur), from where he continued to collect and to send home the species he did not recognise, notably to William Hooker in Glasgow.

During this time Wight employed local men to bring him specimens, and by 1830 at least, employed 'an artist, a collector for supplying him and myself with plants procurable in the vicinity, & another with his assistant, for collecting at a distance'. The artist at this time was probably Rungiah. There are two main ways in which Wight's paintings (and specimens) differed from those of earlier botanists such as Roxburgh. Perhaps because of the scarcity and expense of paper (and he financed the work himself in his spare time) he used smaller sheets of paper, closer to quarto than the usual folio, and secondly, he determined to publish the paintings and descriptions himself.

In using smaller sheets of paper for the paintings, he may have been basing his work on Sowerby and Smith's *English Botany*, which was a narrow quarto and published in around 40 volumes between 1790 and 1863. We know that Wight sent five of Rungiah's drawings to Sir William Hooker in 1828, and more in the following years. Some of these were published in various journals, until 1840 when Wight began to publish his own work.

On being transferred from Negapatam, Wight organised leave in

England, and took the chance not only to study and distribute his own specimens, but to study those that had been collected by Wallich, who was then also working in London, and had just published the first volume of his own *Plantae Asiaticae Rariores*, subsidised by the Company. While visiting his family in Scotland, Wight took the opportunity of staying with Hooker in Glasgow, and learning the craft of lithography, which he was to use for his own publications in Madras. From around 1821, lithography replaced engraving as the preferred method for the reproduction of botanical paintings. It was much quicker and cheaper than engraving on copper, and in skilled hands produced subtle and beautiful outlines suitable for hand-colouring.

Wight returned to Madras in 1834, to be surgeon to the 33rd Madras regiment, which took him to various stations including Palamcottah and Courtallum (Courtallam), with its lush tropical vegetation, but was soon appointed to a more botanical job, to investigate the agriculture and natural resources of Madras. This included studying the failure of attempts to grow American tobacco and cotton, as well as the study of successful crops and local products. All this time he collected more specimens and worked on the drawings and text for his books, including a particularly successful visit to the Nilgiri Hills in 1845. As soon as Wight became more settled, in around 1837, he bought his own lithographic press and began the reproduction of Rungiah's paintings.

Wight was unusual among the Scottish botanists in the credit he gave to his artists. By the mid-1830s Govindoo had joined Rungiah as the second of Wight's artists. Rungiah was particularly important, as he was probably painting for Wight as early as 1826 and not only stayed in Wight's employment while he was on leave, but influenced others in the art of botanical illustration, notably Haramanis de Alwis, founder of a dynasty of botanical artists, who worked for George Gardner in Peradeniya in Ceylon. Little is known of Rungiah's background, but it seems likely that he came from the school of painting based at Tanjore.

The Maharajah of Tanjore, Serfoji II (1777–1832), who ruled from 1798 until his death, was a particularly intellectual and enlightened prince: a book collector and an expert ophthalmologist. He kept his own menagerie, and gave an album of bird and animal paintings to Benjamin Torin, the Company Resident at his court. On return to Britain, Torin presented the album to the Company's library: the animal drawings are now in the British Library, but 19 plant drawings, of which only one has since been located, went to the Royal Botanic Gardens, Kew with the dispersal of the India Museum in 1879. Three of Serfoji's albums of flower paintings remain in his extraordinary

personal library which is preserved in the Thanjavur Sarasvati Mahal Library. They were described by the Irish traveller Viscount Valentia in 1804, and have recently been studied again by Savithri Preetha Nair. Rungiah continued to paint for Wight until 1846, and was succeeded by Govindoo, whose work is somewhat less sophisticated. After Wight left India, Govindoo continued to make botanical paintings for Hugh Cleghorn and later for Cleghorn's successor as Madras conservator of forests, Richard Henry Beddome.

Wight retired in 1853 to a large house in Grazeley, a village near Reading, where he occupied his retirement cultivating his garden and keeping a small farm, until his death nine years later. The original paintings by Rungiah and Govindoo are dispersed between various botanical libraries, notably the Royal Botanic Gardens, Kew, the Royal Botanic Garden Edinburgh, and the Natural History Museum, London.

Wight's successor in Madras was Hugh Cleghorn, who continued to employ Govindoo to draw new or unfamiliar plants. Cleghorn also commissioned copies of other illustrations, notably from Roxburgh's collection and from *Hortus Malabaricus*. He collected botanical prints from other publications and had copies made, some from Redouté, others from *Curtis's Botanical Magazine*. In addition to native south Indian species, many of his illustrations show plants from botanic gardens, which gives a record of what was being grown in south India in the mid-19th century. The Australian Moreton Bay chestnut *Castanospermum australe*, for example, was already growing in the Lal Bagh in Bangalore.

Cleghorn's Indian career was a varied one. His initial posting, in 1842, was as a Company surgeon in Madras but was soon transferred to Mysore, based in Shimoga. Later he worked in Madras and became professor of botany, materia medica and therapeutics in the Madras Medical College, and secretary of the Agri-Horticultural Society, where he worked on the great Madras Exhibitions of 1855 and 1857. From 1856 he was appointed conservator of forests for the Madras Presidency, which involved surveying the teak forests of the Western Ghats as far north as Goa. Cleghorn's first tour as conservator took him from the Anamalai Hills to north Canara, as well as visiting Ootacamund and the forests on the east coast. From 1861 until 1864 Cleghorn's forestry work took him to northern India, and in his final tour he acted as inspector-general of forests, before returning to Scotland in 1867 to manage his family estate. Most of Cleghorn's collection of paintings are now in the Royal Botanic Garden Edinburgh.

yellow oleander

Cascarbela thevetia also called *Thevetia peruviana* (Apocynaceae)

Probably by Rungiah, for Robert Wight, 1827.

Native of Mexico and central America, but commonly cultivated all over the tropics as an ornamental or a hedge. The whole plant is very poisonous, but still the bark or leaves are used as an emetic; oil from the seeds kills bacteria and is used to treat skin diseases.

←

pride of India

Lagerstroemia speciosa (Lythraceae)

Probably by Rungiah, for Robert Wight, 1825–28.

This showy species, which can form a large tree to 40 m, is found mainly in southern India and Indo-China, and is the state flower of Maharashtra. A tea made from the leaves is said to treat diabetes; the timber is valuable for veneers and furniture. It is related to the common *L. indica*, the crepe myrtle, a popular ornamental garden shrub or small tree, native of China, so-called because the flowers are wrinkled when in bud, like crepe paper.

sacred barna

Crateva adansonii subsp. *odora* (Capparaceae)

Probably by Rungiah, for Robert Wight, 1825–28.

Part of this painting was redrawn in Glasgow for Hooker's *Icones Plantarum* tab. 178 (1837), (above, right). The generic name commemorates Crataevus, a Greek herbalist, famous in Classical times as a botanical artist, whose work was said to be the basis of the Byzantine *Codex Vidobonensis*, now in Vienna. Some species of *Crateva*, notably *C. religiosa* are used medicinally in India.

yellow silk cotton tree →

Cochlospermum religiosum (Bixaceae)

By Rungiah, for Robert Wight, *c.* 1820.

This drawing was taken to Glasgow by Wight and engraved for W.J. Hooker and published in *Botanical Miscellany 2*, supplement plate 18 (1831). The flowers, especially of the double form, are used as temple offerings.

sensitive plant
Mimosa pudica (Leguminosae)

Probably by Rungiah, for Robert Wight, 1825–28.

This plant grows as a weed in many places in the tropics, but is also cultivated as a curiosity, because the leaves collapse and close up when the plant is touched, and at night. It is easily grown from seed, and makes a small shrubby plant.

→
derris
Derris trifoliata (Leguminosae)

Probably by Rungiah, for Robert Wight, 1825–28.

Wight's specimen of this species is in the herbarium at Kew and this plate was used by William Hooker in *Botanical Miscellany* in 1833. *Derris trifoliata* is a very widespread climber, found from East Africa to eastern China and northern Australia, mostly near the coast and on the margins of mangrove swamps. In India, it is used as insecticides and in medicine; the roots and leaves contain rotenone, a particularly potent fish poison.

rosary pea, crab's eye or gunja

Abrus precatorius (Leguminosae)

Probably by Rungiah, for Robert Wight, 1825-28.

This is a somewhat shrubby climber, well-known for its beautiful seeds, which are very hard, bright red and black. They are used in necklaces and as prayer beads, but are very poisonous if eaten: one seed is said to be fatal to humans, and the crushed seeds were used for making poison darts to kill cattle. Other parts of the plant, such as leaves and roots are used medicinally for a large number of ills, but should not taken without proper supervision.

←

mocche, averaykai, lablab or hyacinth bean

Lablab purpureus (Leguminosae)

Probably by Rungiah, for Robert Wight, 1825-28.

This beautiful bean probably originated in India or Africa, and is now grown throughout the tropics. It forms a strong-growing climbing plant, originally perennial and resistant to drought. Numerous varieties are now cultivated, with flowers, pods and beans of different colours; the leaves are edible raw or boiled; the ripe beans of most varieties are poisonous until well-cooked.

agati or corkwood tree
Sesbania grandiflora
(Leguminosae)

Probably by Rungiah, for Robert Wight, 1830.

This beautiful shrub or small tree is found throughout the warmer parts of India. The flowers, which can be red, white or pink are edible, and the leaves and young pods are also used in curries.

This is a typical partly-coloured drawing, the coloured parts used as a guide for the colourist of the final printed version.

fungus root
Balanophora fungosa subsp. *indica*
(Balanophoraceae)

Probably by Govindoo, for Robert Wight, 1845.

These fungus-like *Balanophora* flowers are found emerging from a solid tuber among leaves on the forest floor, and are parasites on the roots of various trees: the plants have male flowers around the base of the inflorescence (open in the painting), female flowers towards the apex, or the plants can be all male and all female. This plant is common in shola (valley) forests in south India and can be a weed in tea and coffee plantations. It is sometimes eaten or used medicinally by local people in the hills in Kerala.

sea purslane
Sesuvium portulacastrum (Aizoaceae)

Probably by Rungiah, for Robert Wight, 1825–28.

This is a creeper, common in the tropics on sandy seashores, rocks and saltmarshes, often associated with mangroves. The plant is tolerant of salt, is edible and has some medicinal benefits.

This painting was used for an engraving in the *Companion to the Botanical Magazine* 2: t. 23 (1836).

water snowflake
Nymphoides indica (Menyanthaceae)

Probably by Rungiah, for Robert Wight, 1825–28.

This is a small, waterlily-like plant, found floating in pools, lakes and slow rivers in south India; it is now a common weed in rice fields and lakes throughout the tropics. The petals, which are white with a yellow base, are covered with very delicate, white hairs.

tamarind tree, dakkar
Tamarindus indica (Leguminosae)

Probably by Rungiah, for Robert Wight, 1825–28.

Though probably a native of Africa, the tamarind tree has been grown in India since ancient times, and is now found in woodland and along rivers, as well as being revered in villages where old, gnarled trees are a feature of cemeteries. The seeds are edible and the sweet and acid pulp around the seeds can be eaten fresh or used as a paste; they are an important flavouring in Indian cooking around the world. The young leaves are also eaten and the timber is used for furniture and building.

Himalayan indigo →
Indigofera heterantha as *I. pulchella* (Leguminosae)

Hand-coloured lithograph by Dumphy, after a painting by Rungiah, for Wight's *Spicilegium Neilgherrense*, plate 55 (Madras, 1846).

This shows a printed plate, fully coloured, ready for publication, as referred to on page 182. The partially coloured drawing is in the Royal Botanic Garden Edinburgh. *Indigofera heterantha* is a popular garden shrub, found wild from Afghanistan and India to western China.

Ochna squarrosa sometimes called *Discladium squarrosum* (Ochnaceae)

Probably by Rungiah, for Robert Wight, 1825–28.

This forms a large shrub or small tree, with numerous bright yellow, scented flowers clustered along the branches, followed by greenish fruit, ripening to black. It grows mainly in eastern India and Bangladesh; bark and leaves are used medicinally.

→

Ipomoea staphylina as *I. racemosa* (Convolvulaceae)

Hand-coloured lithograph by Dumphy, after a painting by Govindoo.

This beautiful climber grows in the forests of Tamil Nadu and Kerala, and flowers in winter and early spring. J. Dumphy, who lithographed many of Rungiah and Govindoo's drawings for Robert Wight, worked for the Government lithographic press in Madras, but apart from this, little is recorded about his life or circumstances.

BOTANICAL ART IN INDIA TODAY

DESPITE THE LONG TRADITION OF PAINTING IN INDIA, THERE appears to have been a period in the late 19th and early 20th centuries when the depiction of flowers and plants in the style of 'botanical illustration' was not a flourishing activity. There were several reasons for this, among them the inability of artists to attract commissions or steady employment, firstly after the loss of patronage available at the courts of the Mughal emperors and the Deccani, Pahari and Rajput rulers, and then again when the surgeons and botanists of the Company, who had employed many skilled artists, finally left the continent.

In the absence of this financial support, many highly skilled painters, often trained in the traditional style of the miniaturists (which in addition to painstaking brushwork taught many of the skills, such as careful observation and attention to detail, essential for the botanical artist) turned to working mainly for the tourist market. One of the many attributes of the artists of Jaipur, for example, is copying the works of earlier artists, which is regarded as a completely legitimate form of artistic endeavour. Sometimes this can be seen in contemporary paintings that are superficially in the style of a Mughal miniature but with an added flavour. For further reading on this point, see the excellent and informative essays in catalogues published by the Hunt Institute, based in the USA.

Fortunately, in comparatively recent times there has been an international revival of interest in botanical illustration and flower painting, and once again there are some very talented Indian artists working in this field.

There is space here to list just a few of them.

tiger lily
Lilium lancifolium (Liliaceae)

By Thakur Ganga Singh.

This lily is wild in China and Korea where it is common and frequently cultivated for its edible scaly bulbs, and for its edible flowers.
Shirley Sherwood Collection.

THAKUR GANGA SINGH

Thakur Ganga Singh (1895-1970) was awarded the honorary title of Rai Sahib in 1944, in recognition of his contribution to fine art while he worked for 30 years as an artist at the Forest Research Institute in Dehradun. In 1931 he took a year's leave in order to undertake further training at the Slade School of Fine Art, London. In addition to his work at the Institute, Singh also enjoyed the patronage of a number of British officers and their wives, including Lady Willingdon, wife of the 22nd Viceroy of India; her collection of Singh's paintings was brought back to England.

In 1942, he was appointed court painter to Yadavindra Singh, Maharaja of Patiala, a keen amateur botanist with a special interest in the flora of the Simla Hills. He produced over 400 watercolours as illustrations for a book planned by the Maharaja, a project that sadly remained unfinished at the time of the latter's death in 1972.

rhododendron
Rhododendron wightii (Ericaceae)

By P.N. Sharma in 1993.

Joseph Hooker collected this rhododendron in Sikkim in 1850 and named it after Robert Wight. It is common in many areas from Nepal and Bhutan to southern Tibet, usually growing in quantity at around 3,750 m. Sharma's painting is enlarged and adapted from the original plate in Hooker's *Rhododendrons of the Sikkim Himalaya* (1849–51), which was itself adapted by W.H. Fitch from Hooker's field sketch, made in Sikkim. Shirley Sherwood Collection.

P.N. SHARMA

P.N. Sharma (b.1922), a student of Thakur Ganga Singh, worked as an artist in the Forest Research Institute, Dehradun from 1946 until 1980, and, with T.G. Singh, was instrumental in creating a fine collection of watercolours and ink drawings. Illustrations by both Sharma and Singh were published in books such as R.N. Parker's *Common Indian Trees and How to Know Them* (Dehradun, 1933; reprinted 1999), in which the species are illustrated by elegant line drawings.

THE SHARMA FAMILY

Several members of this family, born and based in Jaipur, Rajasthan, specialise in botanical paintings, having been taught the techniques of traditional Indian miniature painting. Works by the three artists listed here have all been exhibited at the Hunt Institute, Pittsburgh, USA.

Ramesh Chandra Sharma (b.1948) works in gouache, tempera and watercolour; his work has also been exhibited at the Commonwealth Institute, London. His brother, Suresh Chand Sharma (b.1951) benefited from a similar training, while Vijay Kumar Sharma (b.1962), taught by his uncle, Ramesh, has produced excellent paintings of bonsai trees, one of which is in the Shirley Sherwood Collection. Further details of their work can be seen in the catalogues of the Hunt Institute for Botanical Documentation, Carnegie Mellon University, Pittsburgh, USA.

Bonsai
Possibly *Juniperus chinensis*. (Pinaceae)

By Vijay Kumar Sharma.

An ancient tree, called yamadori when collected from the mountains, grown in a pot and trained to emphasise its age. The art of bonsai is an ancient tradition in Japan, introduced from China. The white half-dead twisted wood of the trunk is a valuable feature of a juniper bonsai.
Shirley Sherwood Collection.

DAMODAR LAL GURJAR

Damodar Lal Gurjar (b.1958) graduated from Rajasthan School of Arts, Jaipur, in 1981, and currently works as a freelance artist in Jaipur. His work is influenced by the traditional school of painting, and he uses gouache, oil, tempera and watercolour. In 2001 he had a solo exhibition at the Hunt Institute for Botanical Documentation, Pittsburgh. His subjects include birds and vegetables, but he is particularly noted for his paintings of bonsai. His paintings have been exhibited in Washington DC and New Delhi, and are in the Shirley Sherwood Collection.

nasturtium, Indian cress
Tropaeolum majus (Tropaeolaceae)

By Damodar Lal Gurjar.

This is a creeping annual, introduced to India from Peru, probably in the 17th century and commonly grown as an ornamental annual. Both flowers and leaves are edible, and have a cress-like flavour. Shirley Sherwood Collection.

MAHAVEER SWAMI

Mahaveer Swami (b. Bikaner, Rajasthan) received his initial training at home, and later at the Rajasthan School of Art, Jaipur. He studied traditional techniques under guidance of his mentor, the late Shri Vedpal Sharma 'Bannu', in a studio that is over 300 years old. Mahaveer specialises in paintings of flowers, animals and scenes of ancient and modern Indian life in the style of Indian miniatures.

    He grinds his own colours from rocks such as coral, malachite and lapis lazuli, some of which he has inherited, producing subtle colours, and he also uses a smooth agate stone to press the surface of the paper, a technique which can also be seen in the work of the 18th century botanical painters. As well as paper, he paints on silk, using background wash and tempera for the final details, and

pitcher plant
Nepenthes rafflesiana
(Nepenthaceae)

By Mahaveer Swami.

This pitcher plant is found wild in many parts of South-East Asia, growing on cliffs and openings in forest. It is named after Sir Stamford Raffles (1781–1826), founder of Singapore, and a keen collector of paintings of plants, birds and other animals. The artist developed this painting in the garden of the Botanical Survey of India, Shillong in Meghalaya.

sacred lotus

Nelumbo nucifera (Nelumbonaceae)

By Mahaveer Swami.

The sacred lotus is widely cultivated in lakes and ponds. The bluish-green round leaves are held above the water; the thick rhizomes and leaves are both edible.

a dry brush technique with squirrel hair for the final details of plant portraits.

His botanical paintings are very diverse in character, some studies from life or naturalistic images taken from other paintings, others stylised and reminiscent of Mughal decorative and imaginative flower paintings or floral borders.

He has exhibited widely in India and around the world. His artworks are held in the Hunt Institute for Botanical Documentation in Pittsburgh, and also represented in many private collections. He was one of the Rajasthani artists who illustrated *The Garden of Life: An Introduction to the Healing Plants of India*, by Naveen Patnaik (New York, 1993).

musk melon

Cucumis melo (Cucurbitaceae)

By Mahaveer Swami.

ARUNDHATI VARTAK

Arundhati Vartak (b.1960, Shivajinagar), studied psychology and Marathi literature at Bombay University. Inspired by Indian miniature paintings, she is known particularly for her depictions of Indian trees, and works in an unusual style, employing some of the technique of a miniaturist but in a modern, dramatic and vibrant style, using poster colours on paper to capture the essence of each tree. While not strictly botanical, her eye-catching works show something of the Indian reverence for trees, and are based on numerous detailed sketches. Exhibitions of her work have been held at the Hunt Institute of Botanical Documentation, and at Chatham College Art Gallery, Pittsburgh, USA, as well as in Bombay, and her paintings are in a number of private collections.

Indian coral tree

Erythrina variegata (Leguminosae)

By Arundhati Vartak.

This striking tree usually flowers on bare branches in early spring. Some leaves and seed pods are shown here, and an Indian house crow is seen sipping nectar from the flowers. Shirley Sherwood Collection.

red apples
Malus cultivar (Rosaceae)

By Jaggu Prasad.

Exhibited at Hunt Institute International Exhibition (1992). Shirley Sherwood Collection.

←
cannonball tree
Couroupita guianensis (Lecythidaceae)

By Arundhati Vartak.

This large tree originates in the tropical forests of South America, but is now common in the warmer parts of India. The sweetly-scented flowers are hooded like a snake, and the trees are often planted by Shiva temples. The hard fruit, which gives the tree its usual name, can be 20 cm across. Shirley Sherwood Collection.

JAGGU PRASAD

Jaggu Prasad was born in Jaipur, Rajasthan in 1963. He was taught traditional Indian and botanical painting from a young age by the influential artist Padamshree Kripal Singh. He is best-known for his remarkable paintings of fruit and vegetables for which he uses gouache and watercolour, and his trompe l'oeil images of natural history books. His work was included in the Hunt Institute's 7th International Exhibition of Botanical Art and Illustration in 1992.

HEMLATA PRADHAN

Hemlata Pradhan was born in 1974 in Kalimpong, Darjeeling, West Bengal, where her family owns a plant nursery, and where she continues to live and work as a botanical illustrator. She received her first lessons in drawing at school, and took a first degree in graphics (printmaking); in an interview for an online Plant Sciences Portal [Indian Botanists, Monday 2 June 2014], she noted that at that time there was no course locally available in natural history illustration 'which is indeed sad because India, once upon a time, had a rich legacy of many wonderful and proficient plant and animal illustrators.'

    Hemlata has a diploma in Botanical Illustration from the Royal Botanic Gardens, Kew, where she was taught by Christabel King and Judy Stone, and an MA in Natural History Illustration and Ecological Studies from the Royal College of Art, London. In 1999 she was awarded a Gold Medal by the Royal Horticultural Society, London,

orchid

Diplomeris hirsuta (Orchidaceae)

Watercolour drawing by Hemlata Pradhan.

A delicate, dwarf orchid growing on shady sandstone rocks in grassy places and forest at low altitudes in Nepal, Sikkim, Bhutan and possibly also in south-west China. The flowers, around 3 cm across, appear from June to August. Hemlata's painting shows it growing with *Utricularia* sp. *Begonia* sp., *Selaginella* and ferns.

and in 2005 her paintings of India's wild orchids earned her another Gold Medal at the 18th World Orchid Conference in Dijon. Hemlata has worked with many botanists and is involved with the work of the Orchid Specialist Group/ International Union for Conservation of Nature/ Species Survival Commission.

In 2003, with initial support from Lady Sainsbury, Hemlata founded the Himalayan Trust for Natural History Art in Kalimpong, a charitable trust established to combine art, education and conservation. At the time of writing, a programme is running to teach a group of talented local children, aged 7-14, to learn how to observe and draw natural history subjects. The pupils enjoy the advantage of familiarity with the local flora and fauna, and are encouraged to improve their powers of observation and attention to detail by keeping sketchbooks and documenting their work in diaries.

orchid

Dendrobium jenkinsii (Orchidaceae)

Watercolour drawing by Hemlata Pradhan.

A beautiful dwarf epiphyte growing in open forests, usually on deciduous trees, at 700 to 2,000 m, from Sikkim and Bhutan to S. Yunnan and Hainan. The flowers are around 3 cm across, produced in early spring.

BOTANICAL ART IN INDIA TODAY

orchid
Pleione praecox (Orchidaceae)

Watercolour drawing by Hemlata Pradhan.

A small deciduous orchid, found from Uttar Pradesh and Nepal to north Vietnam and Yunnan, growing on mossy tree trunks, rocks and steep banks in the forest at up to 2,500 m. The flowers appear in late autumn, before the new leaves emerge.

→
orchid
Calanthe masuca (Orchidaceae)

Watercolour drawing by Hemlata Pradhan.

A very widespread species, found from Nepal to Yunnan, Hong Kong, Java, Sumarta and Borneo, growing in mossy places in temperate woods.

BOTANICAL ART IN INDIA TODAY 215

pride of India
Lagerstroemia speciosa
(Lythraceae)

Watercolour drawing by Nirupa Rao from *Pillars of Life* (Mudappa *et al*. 2018).

This spectacular flowering tree is grown throughout the warmer parts of India; it is interesting to compare Nirupa Rao's painting, which shows the typical frilly petals of *Lagerstroemia* with the stiffer scientific style of Rungiah, working for Wight, on page 186.

NIRUPA RAO

Based in Bangalore, south India, Nirupa Rao (b.1990) initially studied social sciences at Warwick University, England, before following an online course in botanical illustration with English artist Elaine Searle. Nirupa has worked with the Mysore-based Nature Conservation Foundation, using watercolours to illustrate the native trees of the south Indian rainforest in a book entitled *Pillars of Life: Magnificent Trees of the Western Ghats* (2018). She recently published *Hidden Kingdom: Fantastical Plants of the Western Ghats* with text by Suniti Rao, research by Siddarth Machado and Prasenjeet Yadav, supported by the National Geographic Society.

Bhesa indica (Centroplacaceae)

Watercolour drawing by Nirupa Rao from *Pillars of Life* (Mudappa *et al.* 2018).

Bhesa is a genus of seven large evergreen trees, mainly in tropical eastern Asia, from Nepal, India and Sri Lanka to Thailand, Indonesia and New Guinea. *B. indica* is a rare tree in wet evergreen valley (shola) forest in the Western Ghats. The seeds have a fleshy aril which is eaten by fruit bats.

flame-of-the-forest, dhak tree or pâlāsh

Butea monosperma (Leguminosae)

Watercolour drawing by Nirupa Rao from *Pillars of Life* (Mudappa *et al.* 2018).

This tree is found across India and South-East Asia, as far east as Indonesia, flowering in spring before the new leaves open. The flowers make the saffron-coloured palash powder, used as dye at holi, and sold for medicine. The tree has many other traditional and culinary uses. Nirupa Rao's spectacular painting shows the crowded flowers and seed pods typical of this tree. Compare this with the early 19th-century painting, possibly by Sheikh Zain al-Din on page 28.

oakleaf fern

Drynaria quercifolia, sometimes called *Aglaomorpha quercifolia* (Polypodiaceae)

Watercolour drawing by Nirupa Rao from *Hidden Kingdom* (N. Rao *et al.* 2019).

This striking fern climbs on the trunks and branches of forest trees. Its leaves are of two kinds, normal deeply cut green leaves which arch outwards and stiff lobed, often brown leaves which lie flat against the tree, protecting the roots and trapping debris. Nirupa's painting shows the plant growing on a dead tree in a humid area, with other small ferns and orchids beginning to colonise the branches. Oakleaf fern is found wild from India to northern Australia, and often cultivated in greenhouses and tropical gardens. *Drynaria* rhizomes are also used medicinally to restore bone density.

BIBLIOGRAPHY

SOURCES AND SELECTED BIBLIOGRAPHY

Archer, Mildred. (1962). *Natural History Drawings in the India Office Library.* HMSO, London.

Cathcart, J.F. (1855). *Illustrations of Himalayan Plants: Chiefly selected from drawings made for the late J. F. Cathcart, Esq., of the Bengal Civil Service.* Reeve, London.

Desmond, Ray. (1992). *On the Discovery of the Indian Flora.* Oxford University Press, Oxford.

Desmond, Ray. (1994). *Dictionary of British & Irish Botanists and Horticulturists.* Revised edition. Taylor & Francis and the Natural History Museum, London.

Grierson, A.J.C. & Long, D.G. *et al.* (1983-2001). *Flora of Bhutan: Including a record of plants from Sikkim and Darjeeling.* Royal Botanic Garden, Edinburgh.

Hooker, W.J. *et al.* (1836 onwards). *Hooker's Icones Plantarum.* Bentham-Moxon Trust, Kew.

Llewellyn-Jones, Rosie. (1992). *A Very Ingenious Man: Claude Martin in Early Colonial India.* Oxford University Press, New Delhi.

Mudappa, D., Raman, T. R. S., Rao N., and Ghuman, S. (2018). *Pillars of Life: Magnificent Trees of the Western Ghats.* Nature Conservation Foundation, Mysore.

Noltie, H.J. (1999). *Indian Botanical Drawings 1793-1868 from the Royal Botanic Garden Edinburgh.* Royal Botanic Garden, Edinburgh.

Noltie, H.J. (2002). *The Dapuri Drawings: Alexander Gibson and the Bombay Botanic Gardens.* Antique Collectors Club in association with the Royal Botanic Garden, Edinburgh.

Noltie, H.J. (2016). *The Cleghorn Collection: South Indian Botanical Drawings 1845 to 1860.* Royal Botanic Garden, Edinburgh.

Rao, N. & Rao S. (2019). *Hidden Kingdom: Fantastical Plants of the Western Ghats.* Nirupa Rao, Bangalore.

Reede tot Drakestein, Hendrik van. (1678-93). *Hortus Indicus Malabaricus.* 12 volumes. Sumptibus Joannis van Someren, Joannis van Dyck, Henrici and Theodori Boom, Amsterdam.

Robinson, Tim. (2008). *William Roxburgh: The Founding Father of Indian Botany.* Phillimore in association with the Royal Botanic Garden, Edinburgh.

Roxburgh, William. (1795-1819). *Plants of the Coast of Coromandel.* George Nicol, London.

Royle, John Forbes. (1833-40). *Illustrations of the Botany and Other Branches of the Natural History of the Himalayan Mountains and of the Flora of Cashmere.* W.H. Allen and Co., London.

Wight, R. & Hooker, J.D. (ed.). (1831). *Illustrations of Indian Botany, Principally of the Southern Parts of the Peninsula.* Curll & Bell, Glasgow.

Wight, Robert. (1838-53). *Icones Plantarum Indiae Orientalis.* 6 volumes. Madras.

Wight, Robert. (1840-50). *Illustrations of Indian Botany.* 2 volumes. Madras.

Wight, Robert. (1846-51). *Spicilegium Neilgherrense.* 2 volumes. Madras.

Wallich, Nathaniel (1830-32). *Plantae Asiaticae Rariores; or Descriptions and figures of a select number of unpublished East Indian plants.* 3 volumes. Treuttel and Würtz, London.

FURTHER READING

Dalrymple, William (ed.). (2019). *Forgotten Masters: Indian Painting for the East India Company.* Philip Wilson Publishers and the Wallace Collection, London.

Griggs, P. & Endersby J. (2011). *Joseph Hooker Botanical Trailblazer.* Royal Botanic Gardens, Kew.

Hooker, J.D. (2017). *Joseph Hooker's Rhododendrons of Sikkim Himalaya.* Facsimile Edition. Royal Botanic Gardens, Kew.

Kew Pocketbook series. (2019). *Palms.* Royal Botanic Gardens, Kew.

Manilal K.S. (2003) *Van Rheede's Hortus Indicus Malabaricus*. English edition. 12 volumes. University of Kerala, Thiruvananthapuram.

Noltie, H.J. (2007). *Robert Wight and the Botanical drawings of Rungiah & Govindoo,* 3 vols. Royal Botanic Garden, Edinburgh.

North, Marianne & Mills, Christopher. (2018). *Marianne North: The Kew Collection.* Royal Botanic Gardens, Kew.

Payne, Michelle (2016). *Marianne North: A Very Intrepid Painter*. Revised edition. Royal Botanic Gardens, Kew.

Patnaik, Naveen (1993). *The Garden of Life: An Introduction to the Healing Plants of India.* Doubleday, New York.

Reddy, Sita (ed.). (2019). 'The Weight of a Petal: Ars Botanica'*, Marg magazine*, Volume 70 / 2, December 2018-March 2019.

Willis, Kathy & Fry, Carolyn. (2014). *Plants from Roots to Riches.* John Murray, London in association with the Royal Botanic Gardens, Kew.

www.biodiversitylibrary.org – the world's largest open access digital library specialising in biodiversity and natural history literature.

https://www.huntbotanical.org – Hunt Institute for Botanical Documentation, with extensive international botanical art collections.

www.kew.org – Royal Botanic Gardens, Kew website with information on Kew's science, horiculture and collections.

www.plantsoftheworldonline.org – authoritative information on the world's flora from research published over the last 250 years.

INDEX TO PLANT ILLUSTRATIONS & ARTISTS

Abelmoschus moschatus 76
Abrus precatorius 193
Aconitum ferox 64
Actinidia strigosa 176
Aeschynanthus peeli 174
Agapetes variegata 149
agati 194
amaltas 85
amaranth (*Amaranthus hypochondriacus*) 89
Amorphophallus 90, 125
Anacardium occidentale 86
anyaar 139
apple 211
Argyreia cymosa 96
asafoetida 155
Ascocentrum ampullaceum 121
ashwagandha 67
averaykai 192

Balanophora fungosa subsp. *Indica* 195
balsam 140-1
bamboo 157-8
Bearilall 108
Berberis napaulensis
Bergenia ciliata f. *ligulata* 164
Bhesa indica 217
Bistorta affinis, B. vacciniifolia 144
bitter melon 44-5
bohdi or bo tree 116-7
bonsai 205
Boswellia serrata 26
Brijlall 107
bristletips 6
Burmese lacquer 136
Butea monosperma 28, 218

Calanthe 215, 165
candle bush 77
Canna indica 27
cannabis (*Cannabis sativa*) 113
cannonball tree 210
Capsicum annuum 20
cardinal vine 75
Cascarbela thevetia 187
cashew 86
Cassia fistula 85
cat's whiskers 78

Cheniella corymbosa 99
cherry 154, 175
chilli pepper 20
chir pine 150
chrysanthemum 38, 112
cinnamon (*Cinnamomum verum*) 88
Citrus × *limon* 104
clematis 97, 177
Cleome 25, 78
clubmoss 52
Cochlospermum religiosum 189
coriander (*Coriandrum sativum*) 109
corkwood tree 194
Cornus capitata 138
cotton 19
Couroupita guianensis 210
crab's eye plant 193
Crateva adansonii subsp. *odora* 188
Crocus sativus 22
Cucumis 55, 87, 187, 208
cup-and-saucer plant 83
Curcuma 94, 95
Cymbidium elegans 172
Cyrtosia falconeri 162

dahlia (*Dahlia*) 23
dakkar 198
Das, Bhawani 72-3, 79
Dawlat 35
Delphinium denudatum 152
Dendrobium 120, 130, 213
Derris (*Derris trifoliata*) 191
dhak tree 28, 218
Didymocarpus 132, 171
Dillenia scabrella 56-7
Diplomeris hirsuta 212
dogwood 138
Dombeya wallichii 137
Drynaria quercifolia 219

Eriocaulon sexangulare 124
Erythrina variegata 90-1
Ferula narthex 155
Ficus religiosa 116-7

Fitch, W.H. 179-81
flame-of-the-forest 28, 218
fungus root plant 195

ganja 113
Garcinia pedunculata 84
ginger, wild 148
ginseng, Indian 67
Gloriosa superba 74
Gluta usitata 136
Gorachand 56-7, 128-9 132, 138
Gossypium 19
gourd 100-1
Govan, Mrs (Mary) 154-5
gunja 193
Gurjar, Damodar Lal 206

haldi 94
Hedychium coccineum 148
henbane 62
Himalayacalamus falconeri 157-8
Himalayan fan palm 53
Himalayan monkshood 64
hing 155
hogweed 69
Holmskioldia sanguinea 83
Huperzia squarrosa 52
hyacinth bean 192
Hydrocotyle himalaica 68
Hyoscyamus niger 62

Impatiens 140-1, 173
Indian almond 79, 122-3
Indian coral tree 90-1
Indian cress 206
Indian frankincense 26
Indian shot 27
Indian traveller's joy 97
indigo (*Indigofera*) 17, 161, 199
Ipomoea 75, 201
iris 33, 38

jadwar 152
Juniperus chinensis 205
Justicia adhatoda 66

kanak champa 106
Kashmir sage 58
kathi 161
Khan, Muhammad 38
knotweed 144

lablab (*Lablab purpureus*) 192

Lagerstroemia speciosa 186, *216*
Lall, Manu 51, 52
lemon 104
Lilium lancifolium 203
lily 33, 74, 203
lima bean 93
Lithocarpus elegans 135
Lyonia ovalifolia 139

magnolia (*Magnolia*) 134, 170
mahogany, Indian 107
mahonia (*Mahonia napaulensis*) 158-9
Malabar nut 66
Malus cultivar 211
mango (*Mangifera indica*) 42-3
Mansur 31-3
marigold 38
melon 44-5, 55, 87, 208
Mimosa pudica 190
Mir'Ali 35
mocche 192
Mogul-Ian 54
Momordica 44-5, 100
mountain cassia 63
Mucuna monosperma 59
musk mallow 76

Nardostachys jatamans 146
nasturtium 206
Nelumbo nucifera 2, 208
Nepenthes 51, 207
Nicandra physalodes 154
Nymphoides indica 197

oak, evergreen 135
oakleaf fern 219
Ochna squarrosa 200
orchid 120-1, 130-1, 162-3, 165, 172, 212-5
Oryza sativa 92
Oxyspora paniculata 6

Pajanelia longifolia 133
pajneli (*Pajanelia longifolia*) 133
pâlāsh 28, 218
Paphiopedilum venustum 131
Parochetus communis 16
pea 16, 114-5, 145, 193

peach tree 153
peepal tree 116-7
pennywort 68
Phalaenopsis taenialis 163
phanera 99
Phaseolus lunatus 93
Phlomis cashmeriana 58
pimpernel 38
pink ball tree 137
Pinus roxburghii 150
pipewort 124
Pisum sativum 114-5
pitcher plant 51, 207
Pleione praecox 214
Polygala arillata 178
Polystichum squarrosum 160
pomegranate 105
Pradhan, Hemlata 212-5
Prasad, Jaggu 211
pride of India 186, 216
Prunus 153-4, 175
Pterospermum acerifolium 106
Punica granatum 105

Ram Das 49
Rao, Nirupa 216-9
Rheum 70-1, 147
rhododendron (*Rhododendron*) 179, 180-1, 204
rhubarb 70-1, 147
rice 92
rose 38
rue 108
Rungiah 59 , 67, 182-201
Ruta graveolens 108

sacred barna 188
sacred lotus 2, 208
saffron 22
Samlall 107
sandpaper tree 56-7
sea purslane 196
Senna 63, 77
sensitive plant 190
Sesbania grandiflora 194
Sesuvium portulacastrum 196
Sharma, P.N. 204
Sharma, Vijay Kumar 205
shieldfern 160

shoo-fly plant 154
shrubby milkwort 178
sieva 93
Singh, Luchman 58
Singh, Thakur Ganga 203
slipper orchid 131
sohdanei 84
spider flower 25
spikenard 146
Stephania japonica var. *discolor* 54
Sterculia foetida 122-3
Strobilanthes attenuata 151
Swami, Mahaveer 207-8

tamarind tree (*Tamarindus indica*) 198
Terminalia catappa 79
Tetrataenium nepalense 69
Thermopsis barbata 145
toon (*Toona hexandra*) 107
Trachycarpus martianus 53
Trichosanthes tricuspidata
Tropaeolum majus 206
tulip 31, 37
turmeric 94

Vartak, Arundhati 209-10
vasaka 66
vine 54
violet 33
Vishnupersaud 16, 22, 52, 53, 54, 64, 128-39, 142, 145-7, 160

water snowflake 197
wild larkspur 152
Withania somnifera 67
woolly dyeing rosebay 65
Wrightia arborea 65

yam 90, 125
yellow oleander 187
yellow silk cotton tree 189

Zain al-Din, Sheikh 28, 49, 72-8

ACKNOWLEDGEMENTS

The author would like to thank Henry Noltie for his advice and the use of his notes and identifications as well as his published writings; Holly Morgenroth for the introduction to the Cresswell collection; John Hatt for his introductions in India, and their Highnesses the Maharaja and Maharani of Jodhpur and Marwar and Rao Raja Mahendra Singh (Monty) for their hospitality and kindness in Jodhpur and Nagaur; Julia Buckley, Patricia Long, Pei Chu and the Library, Art and Archives staff at Kew for their patient and unfailingly help; Gina Fullerlove for enthusiasm and support for the book, and my wife Alison for continual discussion and help.

Kew Publishing would like to thank Fiona Ainsworth, Julia Buckley, Craig Brough, Pei Chu, Holly Carter-Chappell, Sophie Cooper, Paul Little, Ann Marshall, Divya Mudappa, Holly Morgenroth, Mark Nesbitt, Henry Noltie, Lynn Parker, Michelle Payne, Hemlata Pradhan, Sita Reddy, Nirupa Rao, Martyn Rix, Shirley Sherwood, Mahaveer Swami. Special thanks to Priya Kapoor and the team at Roli Books, New Delhi.

PICTURE CREDITS
(Numbers refer to pages)

31 Aligarh Muslim University/Ebba Koch; 38, 48, British Library Board/Bridgeman Images; 33 Golestan Palace Library, Tehran; 206 Damodar Lal Gurjar; 37 Laddawan Hengtabtim /123RF.com; 36 Igor/123RF.com; 34/35 Jagdish and Kamla Museum of Indian Art, Hyderabad; 216, 217, 218 Nature Conservation Foundation, Mysore; 212-215 Hemlata Pradhan; 211 Jaggu Prasad; 216-219 Nirupa Rao; 28, 74-79 Royal Albert Memorial Museum & Art Gallery, Exeter City Council; 203, 204, 205, 209, 210,211 Shirley Sherwood Collection; 204 P.N. Sharma; 205 Vijay Kumar Sharma; 203 Thakur Ganga Singh; 207, 208 Mahaveer Swami; 209, 210 Arundhati Vartak; 35 V&A Images

All other images are copyright of the Board of Trustees of the Royal Botanic Gardens, Kew.

Every effort has been made to contact and acknowledge correctly the source of copyright holders; the publisher apologises for any unintentional errors or omissions, which will be corrected in future editions of this book.